# 50 WALKS IN

# Cambridgeshire & East Midlands

## 50 WALKS OF 2–10 MILES

First published 2003
Researched and written by Andrew McCloy
Field-checked and updated 2009
by Tony Kelly

Commissioning Editor: Sandy Draper
Senior Editors: David Popey and
Penny Fowler
Designer: Tracey Butler
Picture Research: Liz Stacey
Proofreader: Sandy Draper
Cartography provided by the Mapping
Services Department of AA Publishing

Produced by AA Publishing
© AA Media Limited 2009

A03628

ISBN: 978-0-7495-6287-8
ISBN: 978-0-7495-6319-6

A CIP catalogue record for this book
is available from the British Library.

Visit AA Publishing at theAA.com/bookshop

Cover reproduction by Keenes
Group, Andover
Printed by Printer Trento Srl, Italy

Acknowledgements
The Automobile Association would like
to thank the following photographers,
companies and picture libraries for their
assistance in the preparation of this book.

Abbreviations for the picture credits are as
follows: (t) top; (b) bottom; (l) left; (r) right;
(c) centre; (AA) AA World Travel Library.

3, 9, 16/7, 26/7, 52/3, 72/3, 84/5, 104/5,
130/31, AA/J Tims.

Illustrations by Andrew Hutchinson

Every effort has been made to trace the
copyright holders, and we apologise in
advance for any accidental errors. We
would be happy to apply any corrections in
the following edition of this publication.

Author Acknowledgement:
Many thanks to all the staff of the various
county councils and local authorities who
gave me advice and information during the
research of this book. The National Trust,
English Heritage, Royal Society for the
Protection of Birds and the Woodland
Trust were all very helpful. Special thanks
must go to Frank Inglis of the Forestry
Commission's Northamptonshire division,
Bill Thwaites of Bedfordshire County
Council's Countryside Team, Mary Powell
of Lincolnshire Tourism and Helen
Gamble from the Lincolnshire Wolds
Countryside Service.

On a personal note I would like to thank
Penny Edmonds for her company, her
patience and her first-rate little tent, and
also Jenny McCloy, who at 7½ years old
showed that she can look forward to
a lifetime of enjoyable walking – just so
long as there's an ice-cream van waiting
for her at the end of each trip.

**50** WALKS IN

# Cambridgeshire & East Midlands

50 WALKS OF 2–10 MILES

# Contents

# Contents

## Rating

Each walk is rated for its relative difficulty compared to the other walks in this book. Walks marked ✚✚✢ are likely to be shorter and easier with little total ascent. The hardest walks are marked ✚✚✚.

## Walking in Safety

For advice and safety tips see page 144.

# Locator Map

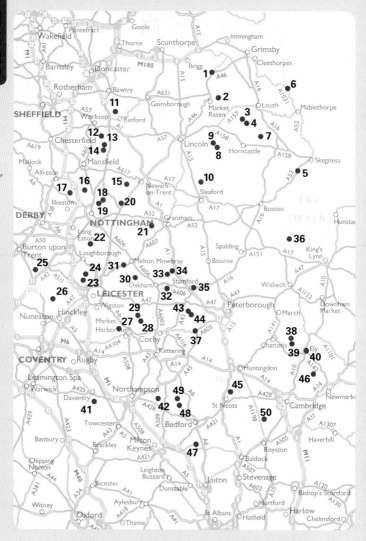

# Legend

| | | | |
|---|---|---|---|
| →⟶ | Walk Route | ▦ | Built-up Area |
| ❶ | Route Waypoint | ▦ | Woodland Area |
| — — — | Adjoining Path | 👫 | Toilet |
| ＼｜／ | Viewpoint | P | Car Park |
| • | Place of Interest | ⊞ | Picnic Area |
| ⌒ | Steep Section | )( | Bridge |

# Introducing Cambridgeshire & East Midlands

Where exactly are the East Midlands? Well, to the east of England's middle is obviously a good start, but where do they actually begin and end? For the purposes of this particular book the East Midlands are loosely defined by Lincolnshire in the north and Bedfordshire and Northamptonshire in the south, Leicestershire and Nottinghamshire in the west, with the welcome addition of Cambridgeshire in the east. Somewhere in the middle of all that lies tiny, exquisite Rutland.

One of the problems with defining the East Midlands is that they are so varied in character – from the dead-flat Lincolnshire coast to Northamptonshire's bold limestone ridges, the steep, wooded slopes of North Leicestershire to the wide flood plain of the River Trent in Nottinghamshire. You can stride out across the chalk whalebacks of the Lincolnshire Wolds or walk below sea level through the Cambridgeshire Fens.

Above all, a tour of the East Midlands confirms its essential Englishness. The elegant stone thoroughfares of Stamford and Oundle have barely changed in hundreds of years, while Ely Cathedral and Southwell Minster will simply leave you open-mouthed. Almost every village has a beautiful medieval church, thatched cottage or an inviting inn, and Northamptonshire seems to have a different stately house at every bend of the road, usually surrounded by landscaped parkland and suitably bizarre follies.

Huge tracts of ancient woodland once covered much of the region, and, although depleted, Rockingham in Northamptonshire and Charnwood in Leicestershire are still worth exploring, while the National Trust's Wicken Fen preserves a tiny piece of original Cambridgeshire fenland. The new National Forest in Leicestershire is emerging to redress the balance, especially poignant since much of the early planting is on the sites of former collieries. In terms of age, little beats the remarkable old oaks of Sherwood, which have seen almost 1,000 years of history, while other locations mark specific events. The Yorkist Richard III lost his crown at Bosworth Field in Leicestershire, and later the English Civil War raged around the region. More recent history is remembered at Lincolnshire's Second-World-War airfields, and we also step out with two of the East Midlands' most notable, but highly contrasting writers – John Bunyan and D H Lawrence.

Rivers play a major part in the make-up of the East Midlands landscape and of course offer splendid walking opportunities – the Nene, Welland, Wreake and Great Ouse all feature in this book. Artificial waterways also

**PUBLIC TRANSPORT**

Local tourist information centres and town halls are generally best placed to give up-to-date details on specific routes and the latest timetables. The UK-wide Traveline is also a useful place to start planning itineraries and connections – for information, call 0871 200 2223 or go to www.traveline. org.uk. For fares and timetable information for national rail services, call 0845 748 4950 or go to www.nationalrail.co.uk.

have their own appeal, and nowhere better than at the Grand Union Canal's impressive lock flight at Foxton. Elsewhere, former quarries (Paxton Pits in Cambridgeshire, Daneshill Lakes in Nottinghamshire) are now first-rate wildlife sanctuaries.

If this hasn't whetted your appetite, try some authentic East Midlands cuisine – real Lincolnshire pork sausages or soft, ripe Leicestershire-made Stilton cheese. Wash it down with a pint of thoroughly English beer from Charles Wells of Bedford, or sample the output from the equally fine Batemans Brewery in Wainfleet, Lincolnshire. Cheers!

# Using this book

### Information panels

An information panel for each walk shows its relative difficulty (see page 5), the distance and total amount of ascent. An indication of the gradients you will encounter is shown by the rating ▲ ▲ ▲ (no steep slopes) to ▲ ▲ ▲ (several very steep slopes).

### Maps

There are 30 maps, covering 40 of the walks. Some walks have a suggested option in the same area. The information panel for these walks will tell you how much extra walking is involved. On short-cut suggestions the panel will tell you the total distance if you set out from the start of the main walk. Where an option returns to the same point on the main walk, just the distance of the loop is given. Where an option leaves the main walk at one point and returns to it at another, then the distance shown is for the whole walk. The minimum time suggested is for reasonably fit walkers and doesn't allow for stops. Each walk has a suggested OS map in addition to the map in the book.

### Start Points

The start of each walk is given as a six-figure grid reference prefixed by two letters indicating which 100km square of the National Grid it refers to. You'll find more information on grid references on most Ordnance Survey maps.

### Dogs

We have tried to give dog owners useful advice about how dog friendly each walk is. Please respect other countryside users. Keep your dog under control, especially around livestock, and obey local bylaws and other dog control notices.

### Car Parking

Many of the car parks suggested are public, but occasionally you may find you have to park on the roadside or in a lay-by. Please be considerate when you leave your car, ensuring that access roads or gates are not blocked and that other vehicles can pass safely.

*Right: Foxton Locks as seen from Rainbow Bridge (Walk 27)*

# North Wolds' Geology

*Walk to the top of the Wolds to unearth
the origins of Lincolnshire's gentle hills.*

---

DISTANCE 6.75 *miles (10.9km)*   MINIMUM TIME *3hrs 30min*

ASCENT/GRADIENT *640ft (195m)* ▲▲▲   LEVEL OF DIFFICULTY ✦✦✦

PATHS *Field paths and country lanes, can be muddy, 1 stile*

LANDSCAPE *Ridge of chalk hills with shallow, grassy valleys*

SUGGESTED MAP *OS Explorer 282 Lincolnshire Wolds North*

START/FINISH *Grid reference: TA 118014*

DOG FRIENDLINESS *Close control near livestock*

PARKING *Public car park behind town hall, Caistor (follow signs)*

PUBLIC TOILETS *By car park*

---

Caistor's origins are Roman, its name Castra meaning camp or fortification, and small fragments of the original encircling wall still remain in the vicinity of the church. Ermine Street passed close by, and a short hillside track joined Caistor to the important north–south route from the Humber to the Roman fort of Banovallum (modern-day Horncastle). Caistor town centre has several impressive Georgian houses, but sadly few from earlier times, since a disastrous fire in 1681 burnt down most of the town.

## Geology and Conservation

Caistor and Nettleton sit at the foot of the sharp western escarpment of the Lincolnshire Wolds, a modest but undulating series of chalk uplands in the county's north east corner, which form the highest land on England's eastern seaboard between Yorkshire and Kent. The high point is Normanby Top, just off the walk, at the dizzying height of 550ft (168m)!

The main rocks of the Wolds – chalk, limestone and sandstone – were laid down during the Cretaceous era around 65 million to 135 million years ago. Overlying sands and gravels came later, during the ice ages of the Pleistocene era, around 1.8 million years ago. Although dominated by a thick band of chalk, the western fringes of the Wolds have deposits of ironstone which was mined during the last century near Nettleton Top. The ore was taken down the hillside and transported by rail to Scunthorpe for smelting. The machinery has disappeared, but the mounds and scars are still evident today.

The high chalk Wolds have poor, thin soils, and are mainly, but not exclusively, grazed by sheep. However, in the south of the Wolds the chalk is covered with deposits of boulder clay, gravel and sand, which give rise to better agricultural soils. Although some villages even had their own brickworks, the chalk has also been quarried for building stone.

The Wolds were designated an Area of Outstanding Natural Beauty in 1973. The Lincolnshire Wolds Countryside Service aims to promote the landscape and its conservation, and improve opportunities for quiet recreation. They produce a regular guide and organise guided walks and events. Visit www. lincswolds.org.uk to find out more.

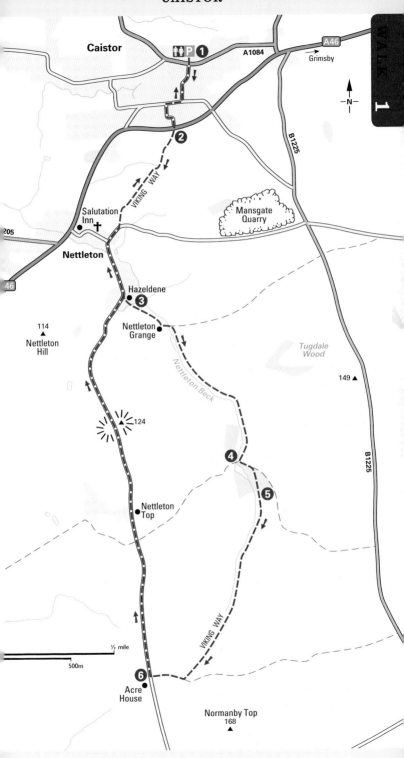

W A L K 1

—N—

Caistor

P 1

A1084

A46 →Grimsby

Mansgate Quarry

B1225

VIKING WAY

2

Salutation Inn

205

Nettleton

46

Hazeldene
3

Nettleton Grange

114
Nettleton Hill

Nettleton Beck

Tugdale Wood

149 ▲

124 ▲

4

5

Nettleton Top

B1225

VIKING WAY

½ mile

500m

6

Acre House

Normanby Top
168
▲

## WALK 1 DIRECTIONS

**1** Walk down the ramp from the car park and cross the road to the Market Place, then continue straight ahead down Plough Hill. At the foot of the hill, turn right along Nettleton Road. When it becomes Richards Row, look for a footpath along a passageway between houses on the opposite side of the road. Now thread your way left through a small estate, all the time following the Viking helmet waymarks for the Viking Way.

### WHERE TO EAT AND DRINK

The Tea Cosy, off Caistor's Market Place, is open daily (except Sun & Mon). The White Hart in Caistor serves good food and beer. The Salutation Inn at Nettleton serves food lunchtime and evening.

**2** Cross over Caistor bypass and go directly ahead through six fields towards Nettleton, veering diagonally left in the last to skirt a modern bungalow. Turn right into the lane below, and walk to the junction in the middle of the village. Go left on Normanby Road. In a little over 0.25 mile (400m), leave the lane for a private drive on the left, indicated 'public bridleway', by a house called Hazeldene.

**3** Follow this route as far as Nettleton Grange, then veer left with the track as it goes through

### WHILE YOU'RE THERE

The walk follows some of the 147-mile (236km) Viking Way that runs north–south along the length of the Wolds. It crosses a region that was occupied by the Vikings from the late 9th century. Beyond the Wolds it loops west, then heads south to finish across the Rutland border.

### WHAT TO LOOK FOR

One of Caistor's more unusual constructions is a brick shed built into the grassy bank at the foot of Plough Hill. It dates from 1869 and once housed the town's horse-drawn fire engine. Apparently the call-out fee was £3 and it was summoned by the tolling of the church bells.

a gate beside the Nev Cole Memorial Stile. On the far side of the gate turn right (the main track goes straight on) and for 0.5 mile (800m) follow a public footpath alongside Nettleton Beck, keeping the stream and ponds on your right. The path, which can be very boggy in places, eventually climbs a rough grassy hillside to emerge on a surfaced lane.

**4** Turn left and walk along the lane uphill for 150yds (137m) until a sign points you right for a track into woodland. Follow the undulating path past bricked-up tunnel entrances, the remains of former ironstone workings.

**5** Go through a gate and cross a stile to emerge onto open pasture and a route that again keeps to the left of Nettleton Beck. When the stream disappears into a spring, continue uphill to reach the final, upper part of the valley. Turn right at the top on to a farm track (bridleway) and walk along to the lane at the end near Acre House.

**6** Turn right, and follow this pleasant lane, via Nettleton Top, all the way back to the village of Nettleton. There are superb views over the flat plain of North Lincolnshire to South Yorkshire and the Humber, with the towers of the Humber Bridge visible on a clear day and the Yorkshire Wolds beyond. At Nettleton retrace your steps back to Caistor.

# Churches of the Wolds

*Explore two beautiful Lincolnshire villages through
their contrasting churches on this quiet circular ramble.*

---

**DISTANCE** 4.25 miles (6.8km)   **MINIMUM TIME** 2hrs

**ASCENT/GRADIENT** 721ft (220m) ▲▲▲   **LEVEL OF DIFFICULTY** ✦✦✦

**PATHS** Field paths, some steep and others muddy

**LANDSCAPE** Undulating chalk hills, deep valleys and woodland

**SUGGESTED MAP** OS Explorer 282 Lincolnshire Wolds North

**START/FINISH** Grid reference: TF 157907

**DOG FRIENDLINESS** On lead near livestock, fine on hedged tracks and lanes

**PARKING** Front Street, Tealby, near tea rooms

**PUBLIC TOILETS** None on route (nearest in Market Rasen)

---

The villages of the Lincolnshire Wolds have many interesting and attractive old churches, and one of the most remarkable is the 'Old Church' of All Saints, situated on a remote hilltop above Walesby. It's 'old' in that it was replaced by a newer version in 1913, and in the succeeding years became dilapidated and rundown. But it was never deconsecrated and, in the early 1930s, a local rambling club began making an annual pilgrimage to the church. Twenty years later the Grimsby and District Wayfarers' Association dedicated the East Window of the Lady Chapel to 'lovers of the countryside', with a stained-glass depiction of walkers and cyclists. Local ramblers still hold an annual service on Trinity Sunday at what is now referred to as 'the Ramblers' Church', and most appropriately the Viking Way long-distance footpath passes through the churchyard.

## Unchanged Since Norman Times

Although repairs have been carried out over the last 20 years to protect All Saints from further weathering and decay, it retains its simple medieval character, a splendid example of what's known as the Norman-Transitional period. Several old, boxed pews remain, while another interesting feature is the old stairway behind the pulpit, which leads to the well-preserved rood loft – the name for the gallery above the rood screen which separates the nave (the main part of the church where the congregation sit) from the chancel (where the clergy and choir sit).

From the church, the glorious views can include the towers of Lincoln Cathedral on a clear day. A Roman villa was unearthed to the east of the church, and a simple Saxon building almost certainly pre-dates the present church (built mainly between the 12th and 15th centuries). Its admirers include John Betjeman, who described All Saints as 'an exceptionally attractive church, worth bicycling 12 miles against the wind to see'.

Down the hill in the village of Walesby, St Mary's is a neat and simple affair by comparison, an example of the Arts and Crafts Movement. The then vicar campaigned laboriously for 30 years to get a new church built in the village, only to drop down dead on the very day that work finally started.

# TEALBY

## The Tennyson Connection

The charming village of Tealby is associated with Alfred, Lord Tennyson, Lincolnshire's very own Poet Laureate. His brother, Charles, was rector at the church for a while, and the impressive 1930s Tennyson D'Eyncourt Memorial Hall is named after another relation.

The parish church of All Saints in Tealby dates from around 1100. It was extensively rebuilt for the Tennyson d'Eyncourts in the 1870s as a shrine to the family – notice the invented heraldry and imitation medieval tombs. The church also houses an impressive collection of more than 100 tapestry 'kneelers' embroidered by local women and depicting people and places from around the village.

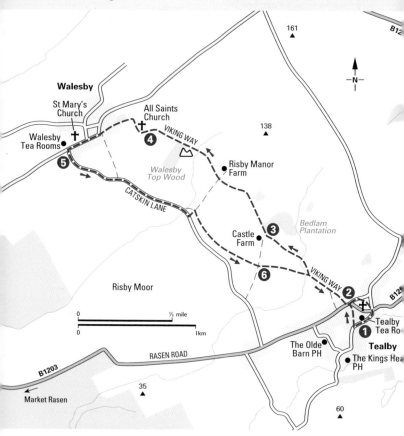

## WALK 2 DIRECTIONS

**1** From the Tealby Tea Rooms walk down Front Street as far as B Leaning & Sons, a butcher and maker of traditional Lincolnshire sausages established in 1860. Turn right into Church Lane, which soon becomes a walkway. At the top, turn left and cross over Rasen Road to follow the public footpath that runs between houses on the opposite side. As far as Walesby you will be following the Norse helmet waymarks of the Viking Way.

**2** Pass through a gate and cross open pasture, aiming for another gate in the far bottom corner. Go through this and along the path ahead, ignoring a footbridge to the left. Walk up the open hillside ahead to reach the corner of Bedlam Plantation which is above Castle Farm.

**3** Turn right and go through a gate for a fenced path beside the woods. At the far end head diagonally left down an undulating grassy field to pass below Risby Manor Farm. Cross the lane leading up to the farmhouse and continue ahead, crossing a deep valley and climbing steeply towards Walesby Top Wood. Pass through a gate and keep straight ahead across a field of crops to reach All Saints Church.

**4** Walk through the churchyard and continue along the Viking Way

as it drops down a wide track into the village. When you reach Rasen Road at the bottom go straight on, past the 'new' parish church of St Mary until you reach the junction with Catskin Lane.

**5** If you need refreshment, cross the road to visit Walesby Tea Rooms. Otherwise turn left and walk along Catskin Lane for 0.75 mile (1.2km). Just past a right-hand curve, turn left at the entrance of a farm drive and go over a cattle grid. This is in fact a public bridleway that leads back up to the hilltop, but you should turn right in a few paces and join a footpath across rough pasture, initially parallel with the road. Stay on this path as it runs along the left-hand side of a field to arrive at the drive to Castle Farm.

**6** The public footpath now continues almost due east across the vast sloping field beyond. When you reach the far side of the field, pass through a gate and drop down to cross a wooden footbridge. Turn right on the far side of the bridge to rejoin the earlier route back into Tealby, this time turning left up Rasen Road to visit All Saints Church. Drop down through the churchyard and follow Beck Hill to the memorial hall, then turn right along Front Street to return to the start of the walk.

DONINGTON ON BAIN

# A Taste for Lincolnshire

*Work up an appetite with this scenic walk through the Wolds west of Louth.*

> **DISTANCE** 6 miles (9.7km)  **MINIMUM TIME** 3hrs
> **ASCENT/GRADIENT** 410ft (125m) ▲▲▲  **LEVEL OF DIFFICULTY** ✦✦✦
> **PATHS** Bridleways and lanes, field paths, may be boggy, 10 stiles
> **LANDSCAPE** Broad, rounded hills and shallow river valley
> **SUGGESTED MAP** OS Explorer 282 Lincolnshire Wolds North
> **START/FINISH** Grid reference: TF 236829
> **DOG FRIENDLINESS** Some livestock, plenty of off-lead potential
> **PARKING** Main Road, Donington on Bain
> **PUBLIC TOILETS** None on route (nearest in Louth)

Lincolnshire is well known as one of the foremost English counties for food production. The fertile soils of the Fens in the south support vast and seemingly endless fields of arable crops, such as potatoes, onions, cabbages and sugar beet (see Walks 8 and 38). The county is the leading producer of cereals and it's also the world's largest producer of daffodils.

A new initiative has been launched within the county to promote Lincolnshire produce. Called 'Tastes of Lincolnshire', its members include tea rooms, B&Bs, pubs and restaurants, as well as many of the local producers themselves. Look out for the stickers and leaflets.

This walk starts and finishes near The Black Horse Inn in Donington on Bain, and there's no better place to try the county's produce after a bracing ramble. The pub specialises in Lincolnshire sausages, traditionally made with coarse ground pork and flavoured with salt, pepper and sage – though other varieties might feature pork with apples or venison with red wine.

In villages and market towns such as Louth, Horncastle, Boston and Spalding, a visit to the local baker will reveal yet another subtle variation of the famous Lincolnshire plumbread, delicious spread with butter and accompanied by a cup of strong tea. Also look out for Grantham gingerbread and Lincolnshire curd tart. Other regional recipes include Lincolnshire dripping cake, traditionally eaten for lunch during harvest time.

Lincolnshire's hand-made poacher cheese has long been famous, and recently sheep's milk products have been reintroduced, with herds of ewes now generating a growing supply of cheese, milk and yogurt. Another return to the county's pastures are Lincoln Reds, a traditional breed of beef cattle with a handsome deep-red coat.

The county is also well-known for haslet – a loaf of cooked, minced pig's offal eaten cold – and chine. Stuffed chine harks back to an 18th-century way of cooking ham, peculiar to Lincolnshire, whereby gashes in the ham are stuffed with parsley, mint, thyme and other herbs before boiling. It is traditionally served cold, sliced, with vinegar and a salad. Finally, don't forget about a drink to accompany all this decent food, and what better than Batemans 'good honest ales', brewed at Wainfleet (see Walk 5).

Burgh on Bain

A157        Louth

Gayton Manor

**5**

**Gayton le Wold**

† Manor Farm

**4**

Pit (Disused)

Grange Farm

123 ▲

Medieval Village (Site of)

**3**

†

**2**

**Biscathorpe**

VIKING WAY

20 ▲

Glebe Farm

Donington on Bain

The Black Horse Inn

†

**1**

River Bain

Pond

**6**

Horseshoe Plantations

151 ▲

82 ▲

Dismantled Railway

MANOR HILL

**A**

**D**

Former Station

**B**

VIKING WAY

**C**

Fox Covert

0        ½ mile
0                    1km

## WALK 3 DIRECTIONS

**WALK 3**

**1** Walk out of the village northwards, past the Norman church and the post office, on to Mill Road. At the first junction turn right, signposted 'Hallington' and 'Louth', then in a few paces go left, over a stile. Walk along the bottom of successive fields, with the River Bain on your left and the lofty Belmont Transmitting Station dominating the skyline further west. After 0.75 mile (1.2km), and having passed a fishing lake, you reach a footbridge.

**2** Cross over the footbridge to reach Biscathorpe's isolated little church, rebuilt in the mid-1800s in a medieval Gothic style. Walk around its perimeter wall, then continue past a house and across a lane to cross another footbridge ahead.

**3** Now head half left across the bumpy outline of a deserted medieval village. The ditches, ridges and mounds give some indication of its layout, and there are more abandoned settlements to the north of the A157 (see Walk 10). Head towards the top of the hill and go through a gate for a path through a small plantation. Turn right on a lane and walk along this for 550yds (503m).

### WHAT TO LOOK FOR

Unless it's misty, you can't miss Belmont Transmitting Station. Built in 1964 by the Independent Television Authority, it was originally 1,265ft (385m) high, which at that time made it the second tallest communications mast in Europe. It then gained a further 7ft (2.1m) when meteorological equipment was added. Since it stands pencil-thin, only 9ft in diameter (2.7m), you feel that all it needs to round it off is a giant flag.

**4** Go over a stile on the right for a signposted public footpath down the side of disused workings, then left across a wide field, aiming for the far corner down by the stream. Go over a footbridge, then follow the farm track round to the left before crossing another footbridge and walking across a meadow to reach the lane at Gayton le Wold.

### WHERE TO EAT AND DRINK

The Black Horse Inn at Donington on Bain (closed Monday) serves four different varieties of local sausages with creamy mash or colcannon (an Irish dish of cabbage and potatoes). Another speciality is Lincolnshire Red beef. Dogs are welcome in the beer garden.

**5** Turn right and walk along the lane past Manor Farm's whitewashed buildings and another miniature church, then out across the hilltop fields. In 0.5 mile (800m), where the lane bends right, go left on a broad track indicated 'public bridleway'. Veer right into the field at the top and follow this obvious and waymarked route alongside huge ploughed fields. (Can you tell what crop is growing?) There are delightful views down across the Bain Valley to your right, back towards Donington. Continue around and above the back of Glebe Farm, by a thick hedge, and go straight over a lane.

**6** In just under 0.5 mile (800m) from the road crossing, turn right where a signpost points to a public footpath downhill behind a hedge. Follow this wide track gradually down via Horseshoe Plantations, then a hedge by fields of grazing horses from the stable near by. Turn right on to the road at the bottom to return to the centre of Donington on Bain.

# A Donington Extension

*Visit a long-abandoned railway and a restored village pond.*
**See map and information panel for Walk 3**

---

**DISTANCE** *8 miles (12.9km)*   **MINIMUM TIME** *4hrs*
**ASCENT/GRADIENT** *443ft (135m)* ▲▲▲   **LEVEL OF DIFFICULTY** +++

---

## WALK 4 DIRECTIONS
### (Walk 3 option)

Where the main route turns right at Point ❻, continue straight on along a wide track across the open hilltop fields. The large communications transmitter ahead to your left is still used by the military, while the huge satellite dishes nearby are a legacy of an early-warning system used in the days of the Cold War.

When you reach Manor Hill (Point Ⓐ) turn right and follow the road all the way to the bridge at the bottom of the hill (Point Ⓑ). It spans the former Louth –Lincoln railway, built in 1876 and eventually closed to passenger traffic in 1951. You can look down over the old station yard and building.

Turn left, towards Stenigot, and walk along the lane to the first junction. Turn right (signposted 'Market Stainton') and after 0.25 mile (400m) go right where a waymark indicates a permissive footpath (Point Ⓒ).

This is the route of the Viking Way long-distance trail, which crosses the edge of fields alongside Fox Covert. Beyond the trees, walk along the left-hand side of a patchy hawthorn hedge to the end (Point Ⓓ).

Here you meet a public footpath, and turn right to follow this back across the dismantled railway. On the far side, where the farm track hairpins off to the farm on the right, go straight on for a clear route across the fields. Stay on this path, crossing four stiles and passing through several gates as you follow the Viking Way waymarks back to Donington on Bain.

As you reach the outskirts of the village make sure you stop to admire the pond on the left, restored by, among others, the Lincolnshire Biodiversity Action Group and students from the Lincolnshire Rural Activities Centre at Kenwick Park.

At the far end, turn right and walk along the lane to emerge opposite The Black Horse Inn. What better place to finish a walk?

> **WHILE YOU'RE THERE**
> The charming market town of Louth is a useful place to pick up some tasty local produce to take home. You can also pick up leaflets on local walks from the tourist information centre in the town hall.

# Wainfleet's Honest Ales

*A short wander around a Lincolnshire market town famous for its brewery.*

| | |
|---|---|
| DISTANCE 3.25 miles (5.3km) | MINIMUM TIME 1hr 45min |
| ASCENT/GRADIENT Negligible ▲▲▲ | LEVEL OF DIFFICULTY ✛✛✛ |

PATHS *Straightforward field paths and lanes*

LANDSCAPE *Flat coastal plain dominated by arable fields*

SUGGESTED MAP *OS Explorer 274 Skegness, Alford & Spilsby*

START/FINISH *Grid reference: TF 498589*

DOG FRIENDLINESS *Take care of traffic on lanes*

PARKING *Market Place, Wainfleet All Saints*

PUBLIC TOILETS *Brook's Walk, opposite Market Place*

## WALK 5 DIRECTIONS

The early growth of Wainfleet, south of Skegness, was the result of a combination of medieval salt-workings and the presence of a safe haven for boats – 'fleet' was once a Roman term to denote a navigable creek.

Facing the Woolpack Hotel by Market Place in the centre of Wainfleet, turn left. Walk along the High Street and over the level crossing, then turn right for a signposted public footpath just beyond Barton Road. This narrow, semi-surfaced route passes a new housing development and, beyond a footbridge, heads out across open fields where staple vegetables such as cabbages and potatoes are often grown. Continue all the way to the far side and turn left on to a lane.

In 75yds (69m) go right on a waymarked footpath along the back of some houses, and finally join the riverside lane which is on the far side of another small field.

Turn right and walk alongside the Steeping River, either on the lane or, better still, on top of the grassy embankment above.

At Crow's Bridge cross over to the road on the south side, and turn left (downstream) on Haven Bank. If you want to lengthen the walk you could continue beyond Crow's Bridge along the right-hand side of Wainfleet Bank for around 0.75 miles (1.2km) before crossing over to the Barkham Arms, a pub that caters mainly for the adjoining caravan park. Near by is the site of the medieval village of Wainfleet, and a footpath across the fields connects with the now isolated St Mary's Church. Return along the opposite bank.

### WHERE TO EAT AND DRINK

The restaurant at Batemans Brewery is open every lunchtime for hearty pub fare and local ales. The Woolpack Hotel serves food every lunchtime and evening, and there is also a fish and chip shop on the High Street.

The quiet lane downstream from Crow's Bridge passes a stretch popular with local anglers, then, after the road veers away from the river through houses and

**WHILE YOU'RE THERE**

The Steeping River issues out into the North Sea at Gibraltar Point. This remote location, reached by a no-through road south from Skegness, is an important National Nature Reserve. Its extensive salt marsh, mudflats and sand-dune system supports a wide variety of wildlife.

a pavement appears, it bends sharply left. Go straight on here, along a narrow walkway between dense hedges, then out behind a row of back gardens. Cross the end of a drive and, after a small fenced strip, emerge on to a road by Halfpenny Hill Cottage.

Turn right, then in 220yds (201m) go left into St Michaels Lane. Walk past the converted stump of an old windmill and, after the last house on the left, turn left between hedges and out across the middle of a field on a popular local path. Continue through a gate and across a meadow, then head half right through the overgrown parkland of Wainfleet Hall. Go out of the gate on the far side and turn left to walk along the pavement of Boston Road back into the town. Just over the bridge you reach Batemans Brewery on the left, off Mill Lane.

The award-winning Batemans Brewery is a must-see for any real-ale lover or pub-goer, and even the non-enthusiast may be surprised at how fascinating the place can be. Established in 1874, Batemans is still run by the same family, and the visitors centre (open daily) has a comprehensible,

step-by-step guide to the brewing process. Discover how a mash tun works, the secrets of wort-cooling, and why the cask-sniffer does what he does. The exhibition also includes a huge collection of beer and pub memorabilia – from a range of traditional pub games, beer mats and posters, to the largest collection of beer bottles in the world. There are organised tours of the brewhouse every afternoon, and in the Windmill Bar you can sample the real thing – or tea and coffee if you prefer.

Continue back along the main road to the railway crossing. On the near side is All Saints Parish Church with its unusual bell turret and, on the far side, turn right into Silver Street. Rounding the far bend you arrive at Magdalen Museum. The impressive, turreted building was built in 1484 for Magdalen College School, and now houses the local library and museum (open each afternoon, except Monday and Wednesday, from Easter to the end of September).

**WHAT TO LOOK FOR**

Barkham Street, near Market Place, was built in 1847 by the Governors of Bethlem Hospital. It's an exact replica of a three-storeyed, terraced row of London houses they had constructed around the hospital in Southwark. Apparently, to cut costs, the design was unchanged for small-town Lincolnshire.

Carry on along what has now become St John's Street, and on past the junction at the end by Market Place to turn left into Barkham Street – and what must surely be the most unexpected encounter on the whole walk (see What to Look For). Turn left at the far end of Barkham Street to return to Market Place.

# On Saltfleet's Dunes

*A wander along the wildlife-rich*
*salt marshes of North Lincolnshire.*

**DISTANCE** 4.75 miles (7.7km)   **MINIMUM TIME** 2hrs 30min

**ASCENT/GRADIENT** Negligible ▲▲▲   **LEVEL OF DIFFICULTY** ✦✦✦

**PATHS** Coastal tracks and field paths, some steps, 3 stiles

**LANDSCAPE** Rolling dunes, open marshland and cultivated fields

**SUGGESTED MAP** OS Explorer 283 Louth & Mablethorpe

**START/FINISH** Grid reference: TF 467917

**DOG FRIENDLINESS** On lead on dunes and marsh between March and August, because of nesting birds

**PARKING** Nature reserve car park at Rimac, off corner of A1031

**PUBLIC TOILETS** At car park and in Saltfleet

A west–east cross-section of Lincolnshire reveals a highly contrasting county – from the agricultural flatlands around Lincoln and Gainsborough to the pleasantly undulating Wolds. However, it's the long North Sea coastline that perhaps holds the most surprises, for if you thought that there wasn't much more to it than funfairs and holiday camps, try this walk for size. It's centred on the Saltfleetby–Theddlethorpe Dunes National Nature Reserve (and try saying that with a mouthful of crisps), an extensive strip of unspoilt beach and marshland that is also a valuable natural habitat for wildlife.

To get a flavour of this peculiar landscape, set aside a few minutes either before or after your walk to explore the short (930yds/850m) Easy Access Trail just to the south of the car park. Information panels explain such fascinating phenomena as 13th-century sand dunes and identify plants such as wild asparagus and bee orchids. Several different habitats make up this nature reserve. The early summer highlight of the bog and freshwater marshes landward of the dunes are carpets of deep pink and purple marsh orchids, and when the temperature rises sufficiently dragonflies and damselflies will take to the wing. The vast rolling dunes are partly covered by clumps of wiry grass and bushes of spiky sea buckthorn, which in autumn are covered by bright orange berries. Meanwhile plants, such as sea lavender and sea purslane, thrive on the salty fringes of the beach, while oystercatchers, with their distinctive black and white plumage and long orange beaks, probe the mud for worms or prise open shellfish.

## Poor Man's Asparagus

The marshes off Saltfleet are famous, in particular, for vast beds of samphire. Also known as glasswort, this small herbaceous annual with thick green stems was once burnt to provide ash for use in the glass-making industry. It used to be called Poor Man's Asparagus, and is still eaten as a starter for a meal. First, you wash and soak it in cold water to remove the saltiness, then boil it for a few minutes in a small amount of water and serve it with lemon

# SALTFLEET

juice and a generous knob of butter. Alternatively, a Lincolnshire variation has it pickled and eaten with chine or boiled bacon.

## Off the Target

It's also worth pointing out that this part of the coast is sometimes used by the RAF for pilot training, and in particular the practice bombing of offshore targets. When this is happening a large red flag will be flying at the end of Sea Lane at Saltfleet, and there will also be red beacons and buoys to cordon off the precise area. It doesn't affect the walk at all, and in fact the event often becomes something of an attraction in its own right, but don't expect to see many birds on those days.

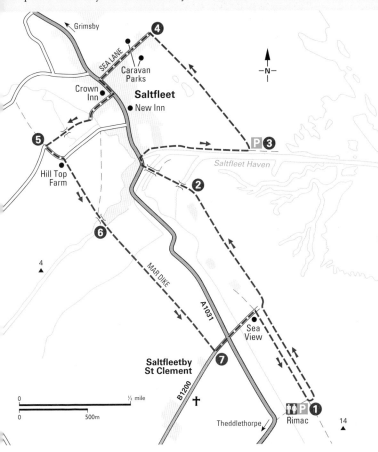

## WALK 6 DIRECTIONS

**1** Walk out of the seaward end of the car park and immediately turn left through a gate, then climb the steps to walk along the top of the dunes with the sea away to your right. Go past Sea View farm and a small parking area and continue beyond a white barred gate, forking right to reach the marshes. Go left and follow the clear track along the edge of the marshes.

**2** At the far end of the dunes, join a rough lane across two successive bridges, then turn right on to the pavement of the coast

*Overleaf: Rimac National Nature Reserve, Saltfleet (Walk 6)*

**WALK 6**

road. After 100yds (91m) cross another small bridge and turn right on to a wide, bumpy lane indicated 'Saltfleet Haven'. Walk along this all the way to the small car park among the dunes – and a bit further if you want to view the sandy bay and river mouth (tide permitting) where seabirds and sometimes seals can be spotted.

**3** At the back of the small car park, and with your back to the Haven, go up the steps and take one of several faint paths through the dunes in order to pick up the wide track that runs just seawards of the vegetation-topped dunes (not along the actual water's edge). The strip of marshes is spread out to your right.

**4** In just under 0.5 mile (800m), turn left up a concrete ramp by some evergreen trees and walk down Sea Lane past the caravan parks. Turn left at the end, then right after the Crown Inn into Pump Lane. At the far end follow

the unmade track as it curves left between houses and, at the gap in the hedge, take the footbridge on the right for a path across fields.

**5** Crossing another footbridge to emerge on the bend of Louth Road, turn left and, just after Hilltop Farm, turn right, across another footbridge, for a long field-edge public footpath.

**6** At the junction of tracks at the far side go straight on, over a small stone bridge across a ditch near a house. Go over the first of three wooden footbridges and continue alongside Mar Dike until you switch banks nearing the far end to reach the road.

**7** Turn left and walk down to the crossroads. Go straight over and along the drive opposite as far as Sea View farm. Turn right on the waymarked public footpath through the farmyard and field beyond, and continue on the clear path along the landward edge of the dunes to return to the car park.

# Belchford and Village Life

*Enjoy an undulating walk through a trio of peaceful villages at the heart of the Lincolnshire Wolds.*

---

**DISTANCE** 7.5 miles (12.1km)   **MINIMUM TIME** 3hrs 30 min

**ASCENT/GRADIENT** 672ft (205m) ▲▲▲   **LEVEL OF DIFFICULTY** +++

**PATHS** Variety of up-and-down field paths and tracks, 8 stiles

**LANDSCAPE** Billowing hillsides, intensively farmed with some grazing

**SUGGESTED MAP** OS Explorer 273 Lincolnshire Wolds South

**START/FINISH** Grid reference: TF 293754

**DOG FRIENDLINESS** Good, but close control around livestock (note stiles)

**PARKING** Lay-by near church on Belchford's main street

**PUBLIC TOILETS** None on route (nearest at Snipe Dales Country Park)

---

This walk is partly based on one of several routes devised by Lincolnshire Wolds Countryside Service and described in a series of attractive colour booklets. Apart from the standard waymarks (yellow for public footpaths and blue for public bridleways), this route is also denoted by occasional green alder-leaf motifs – so there's no excuse for getting lost!

## Contrasting Wolds Villages

Belchford is associated with the South Wold Hunt, whose opening meet traditionally starts outside the Blue Bell Inn. Near the parish church is Chapel Lane, evidence that Belchford's small population also supported two other seats of worship – the Primitive Methodist chapel (built in 1834) and Wesleyan Methodist (1871).

The second village on the route is Fulletby, which used to have an inn, post office, school and bakeries, but is now a quiet little backwater. It's one of the highest villages in the Wolds, and its most famous resident was Henry Winn (1816–1914). Over the course of his long life he was variously the local draper, grocer, churchwarden, schoolmaster and constable. He ran the local post office and established the village library – despite being self-educated, having left school at the age of ten – and earned a place in the Guinness Book of Records for holding the position of parish clerk for an incredible 76 years! In addition, he fathered a total of 21 children, all of them born in Winn Cottage which can still be seen opposite St Andrew's Church off Church Street. Sadly only four of the children (all daughters) survived to adulthood.

## Tetford's Historic Connections

The White Hart Inn in Tetford used to be the meeting place of a gentlemen's literary club, which was once addressed by Dr Samuel Johnson, who is recorded as playing skittles at the inn. Among the club's members was Alfred, Lord Tennyson, who was born in nearby Somersby. Along the street is St Mary's Church, which has the distinction of having the Greenwich Meridian running through its churchyard.

# BELCHFORD

As you head back to Belchford, you will be following a Roman 'salt road', along which salt (that preserved perishables foods) was transferred from the Wash coast at Burgh-le-Marsh to the Roman garrison at Lincoln.

The high, chalk ridge to the north has an even more ancient trackway, the Bluestone Heath Road, probably used in prehistoric times by tribesmen to move animals and perhaps other trading commodities. There are several round barrows dotted along the route.

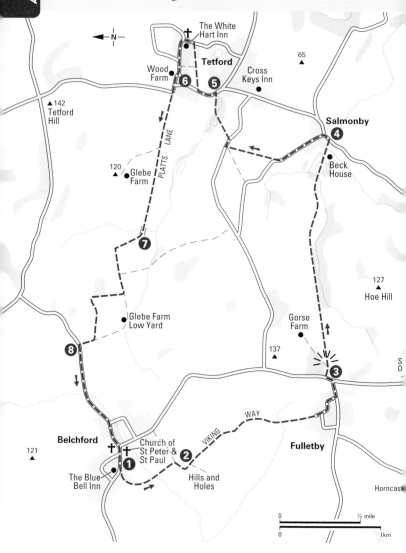

## WALK 7 DIRECTIONS

❶ From the Church of St Peter and St Paul at Belchford, walk west along Main Road and turn left into Dams Lane. At the end

continue through a kissing gate to head left along a fenced path, then uphill beside fields. At the top go right then, after 100yds (91m), go left through a wide gap in the hedge for a path directly uphill.

# BELCHFORD

**②** Continue on this waymarked field-edge route across the hilltop before heading directly south towards the village of Fulletby via undulating pasture. Turn left into the lane then, at the very top, left again to reach the main road.

## WHERE TO EAT AND DRINK

The White Hart Inn at Tetford (closed Monday) is one of the oldest in England and serves filling home-cooked meals, as does the Cross Keys Inn, on the edge of the village towards Salmonby. The Blue Bell Inn at Belchford (closed Monday) also serves food.

**③** Turn left at the T-junction towards Belchford and, after a few paces, cross the road and go over the stile beside the private drive to Gorse Farm for a wonderful view over the southern Wolds. The route now continues almost due east for 1.5 miles (2.4km) down across pasture, then along the bottom of ploughed fields by a strip of woodland. Approaching the far end go through a gate on the right and, skirting the right-hand edge of the small fishing lake at Salmonby, walk along the drive of Beck House to reach the road.

**④** Turn left and follow the road uphill, going left at the junction. After 0.25 mile (400m) turn right

## WHAT TO LOOK FOR

The Church of St Peter and St Paul in Belchford is built from Spilsby sandstone, probably quarried locally, perhaps from a bumpy area to the south of the village known as Hills and Holes (you pass it a few minutes after leaving Belchford). It's often called greenstone since it contains the green mineral glauconite, the colour of which gradually becomes apparent through weathering.

for a field-edge route across to another lane. Turn right, then left on to a path which runs beside a hedge and between a pair of fishing ponds before turning right between woodland and fields to arrive on the road at Tetford.

**⑤** Turn left and walk along West Road for 100yds (91m), then go right, before the holly hedge, on a well-walked path across the wide ploughed field. Walk past the houses on the far side and turn left along East Road past the pub and church. Follow the road around into North Road and along to the triangular junction with West Road at the far end.

## WHILE YOU'RE THERE

Five miles (8km) south of Belchford is Snipe Dales Nature Reserve and Country Park (off the A158/B1195), a wonderful semi-wooded valley rich in wildlife, partly managed by Lincolnshire Wildlife Trust. Short waymarked trails explore the woods, ponds and hillsides – well worth a visit.

**⑥** Go right by Wood Farm for the road out of the village. Where this bends sharply right, beyond the last houses, go straight on along Platts Lane, a wide farm track across fields. Where the main track swings up to the ruined Glebe Farm, go straight on along the field-edge all the way down to a small bridge.

**⑦** On the far side turn right and follow the obvious track up alongside the ditch across open fields. The route then swings left and, after zig-zagging to the north of Glebe Farm Low Yard, it turns right on to the surfaced farm drive to reach the road.

**⑧** Turn left and follow this road back to the centre of Belchford.

# Bardney's Saintly Paths

*An enigmatic outing to the ruined abbeys around Bardney, east of Lincoln.*

| | |
|---|---|
| **DISTANCE** 7.75 miles (12.5km) | **MINIMUM TIME** 4hrs |
| **ASCENT/GRADIENT** Negligible ▲▲▲ | **LEVEL OF DIFFICULTY** ✦✦✦ |

**PATHS** Flat and open arable land, punctuated by woodland

**LANDSCAPE** Easy field paths and bridleways

**SUGGESTED MAP** OS Explorer 273 Lincolnshire Wolds South

**START/FINISH** Grid reference: TF 120694

**DOG FRIENDLINESS** Mostly good, watch for livestock

**PARKING** Horncastle Road, centre of Bardney

**PUBLIC TOILETS** None on route (nearest at Woodhall Spa)

The gentle valley of the River Witham, east of Lincoln, has long been a fertile place, and for more than just potatoes and sugar beet. Once upon a time it housed as many as nine separate monasteries or religious houses, virtually in sight of one another, attracted by the accessibility that the river afforded as well as the ecclesiastical standing of nearby Lincoln.

The first to be built was Bardney, endowed by Ethelred, King of Mercia, and its fame and popularity was sealed when it became the shrine to St Oswald. King Oswald was killed in battle in AD 642 and his body was brought to Bardney – even though his head went separately to Lindisfarne and his arms to Bamburgh. According to the story, Oswald's remains arrived at night, and the monks at Bardney initially refused to allow the cart to enter. Suddenly a 'pillar of light' shone skywards from the coffin, convincing them that this was indeed a saintly person, and after that they never shut their gates. The local Lincolnshire saying for when someone leaves a door open is: 'Do you come from Bardney?'

Whereas the Benedictine monks of Bardney wore black habits, the Premonstratensian monks (from Premontre, in France) at Tupholme Abbey, which is also visited on this walk, wore a white habit and cap and were known as the 'White Canons'. From Matins at 2am through to Compline at dusk, they spent their days in prayer and recitation, although they also found time to rear sheep and sell wool as well as importing building stone via a canal-link to the nearby River Witham. Beyond the solitary remaining wall of Tupholme Abbey is a field where the canons dug their fish ponds.

But like all the other local religious houses, its decline and ruin was swift once the 16th-century Dissolution Act came into force. Before long it was raided for building material and had farm cottages built against it. In 1998, the Lincolnshire Heritage Trust managed to step in and save what was left.

To learn more about Bardney's history, visit the Bardney Heritage Centre (open Thurs to Sun), which opened in the former railway goods shed. There is a tea room in a replica of the old station, exhibitions on Bardney Abbey and RAF IX Squadron, and you can hire bikes to explore the Water Rail Way, a pleasant 31-mile (50km) route beside the River Witham.

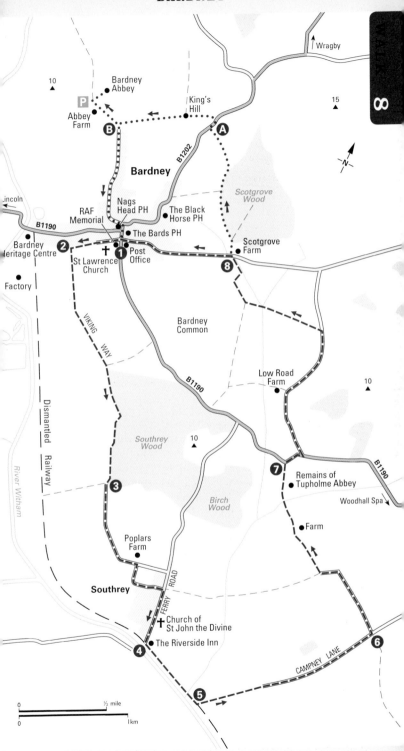

WALK

8

10
▲

Bardney
Abbey

King's
Hill

15
▲

P

Abbey
Farm

B

A

N

B1202

**Bardney**

Scotgrove
Wood

incoln

RAF
Memorial

Nags
Head PH

The Black
Horse PH

B1190

Bardney
Heritage Centre

The Bards PH

2

St Lawrence
Church

1

Post
Office

Scotgrove
Farm

8

Factory

Bardney
Common

VIKING WAY

Low Road
Farm

10
▲

B1190

Dismantled

Southrey
Wood

10
▲

Railway

River Witham

3

Birch
Wood

7

Remains of
Tupholme Abbey

B1190

Woodhall Spa

Poplars
Farm

Farm

**Southrey**

FERRY ROAD

Church of
St John the Divine

4

The Riverside Inn

6

CAMPNEY LANE

5

0              ½ mile

0                      1km

33

## WALK 8 DIRECTIONS

**1** From the RAF memorial opposite Bardney post office, walk along the adjacent Church Lane. Just beyond St Lawrence Church take the public footpath indicated on the left, which squeezes between two fences and turns right along the end of some gardens. (This path can get a little overgrown in the height of summer, in which case follow the road around to the right, past the Methodist chapel, then left on to the main road, turning off left at the sign for the Viking Way.)

**2** At the end of the path turn left on to a wide track through the fields, with the huge British Sugar factory away to your right. Ignore the inviting permissive bridleways into Southrey Wood (left).

### WHERE TO EAT AND DRINK
There are three pubs in Bardney, all serving food. The Black Horse serves lunch from Wednesday to Sunday, while the Nags Head has daily lunchtime specials and The Bards is aimed at families. Food is also available at Bardney Heritage Centre and The Riverside Inn in Southrey.

**3** When the wood finishes continue along the main track, which despite a kink maintains its south-easterly direction. When it reaches the buildings of Southrey it swings left past Poplars Farm. Take the first road on the right (compare the sight of the old thatched cottage with the modern brick-built village hall next door). At the end of the road go right again to reach The Riverside Inn at the far end of Ferry Road.

**4** Turn left on to the raised bank of the River Witham, now part of the Water Rail Way. The overgrown platforms and signs of the former waterside railway station make a strange spectacle, and now you follow the old trackbed beside the river for 650yds (594m).

### WHAT TO LOOK FOR
On a neat green in the centre of Bardney, opposite the post office, is an aviation memorial featuring a gleaming black propeller. There were airfields dotted across Lincolnshire, of course, but this one commemorates the men of IX Squadron who flew Lancaster bombers out of RAF Bardney between 1943 and 1945. Probably their greatest moment was when they sank the German battleship Tirpitz in Norway.

**5** Go left at a public footpath sign and across a footbridge over a drainage dyke for a track across a field. Continue straight on as it turns into a firmer track, then the surfaced Campney Lane.

**6** At the road junction turn left and, after a sharp left bend, turn right on to a signposted public bridleway. Follow this wide grassy ride between hedges. Go through a gate and past a farm to reach the remains of Tupholme Abbey.

**7** Beyond the abbey turn right on to the road, then almost immediately left on to a quiet lane. About 750yds (686m) after Low Road Farm take the public footpath indicated between two fields on the left. The fence is first of all on your right, but when the small dividing dyke appears keep both it and the fence on your left. Go across a small wooden bridge and through another field to turn right on to a cross track all the way to the road.

**8** Turn left for the verge, then pavement back into Bardney.

# The Haunting Outlines of Bardney Abbey

*Add an extra, easy loop to visit the site of Bardney Abbey.*
**See map and information panel for Walk 8**

WALK 9

---

DISTANCE *9 miles (14.5km)*   MINIMUM TIME *4hrs 30min*

ASCENT/GRADIENT *Negligible* ▲▲▲   LEVEL OF DIFFICULTY +++

---

## WALK 9 DIRECTIONS (Walk 8 option)

Leave Walk 8 where it turns left into the road opposite Scotgrove Farm (Point **8**). Go across the road and, keeping to the left of the enormous open barn, go past the farm on a wide track. Immediately before the wooden barrier, turn left on to a wide grassy ride along the edge of the woods. Walk along this very pleasant hedged thoroughfare, with Scotgrove Wood on your right. When the wood finishes carry straight on to reach the road at the end (Point **A**). Turn right, then, a few paces later, cross over for a wide and easy track across open fields, past a mysterious mound known as King's Hill. There are extensive views from here over Lincolnshire's arable flat-lands.

Go straight on at a junction of tracks until, on the far side, you reach the surfaced drive to Abbey Farm (Point **B**). Turn right to follow the road through the farm buildings to reach the parking area for Bardney Abbey at the far side. After the monastery was closed in 1538, it gradually fell into ruin, until in 1909 the local vicar decided to excavate the site. He traced the layout of the cloister, chapter house and so on, and published his detailed findings, but as the weather caused the newly

revealed stonework to deteriorate it was eventually decided to cover up the ruins carefully. You can certainly see the outlines of the buildings and general layout in the field to the right, even if you have to use your imagination a little bit, and an information board gives some useful background.

To return to Bardney simply turn left at Point **B** and follow Abbey Road back through the houses, turning right opposite The Bards to reach the centre.

### WHAT TO LOOK FOR

Bardney Abbey was founded in the 7th century AD, destroyed by Viking raiders two centuries later, then re-established as a monastery in 1087 by Bardney's new Norman owner. The fate of the monks was finally sealed by Henry VIII, and a short-lived local rebellion in October 1536 in their support only led to the execution of several Bardney monks suspected of being behind the unrest. The monastery closed two years later.

# Echoes of Bloxholm's Past

*A gentle stroll near a deserted medieval village north of Sleaford, Lincs.*

---

**DISTANCE** 3 miles (4.8km)  **MINIMUM TIME** 1hr 30min

**ASCENT/GRADIENT** Negligible ▲▲▲  **LEVEL OF DIFFICULTY** ✚✚✚

**PATHS** Wide field tracks and woodland paths, 3 stiles

**LANDSCAPE** Gentle farmland and broadleaved woods

**SUGGESTED MAP** OS Explorer 272 Lincoln

**START/FINISH** Grid reference: TF 065535

**DOG FRIENDLINESS** Mostly good, care needed around livestock

**PARKING** Stepping Out car park, on lane south of Bloxholm

**PUBLIC TOILETS** None on route (nearest in Sleaford)

---

## WALK 10 DIRECTIONS

This easy ramble through the peaceful countryside of mid-Lincolnshire is inspired by one of North Kesteven District Council's excellent 'Stepping Out' walks. They form a series of short waymarked routes that explore the area around Sleaford, south of Lincoln, and take in hidden villages, ancient woodland and medieval castles through to historic RAF airfields. Leaflet guides to all the walks are available in local shops and post offices, or from the tourist information centre in Carre Street, Sleaford.

The walk begins on a lane 350yds (320m) south of the quiet hamlet of Bloxholm, at the designated Stepping Out car park. Facing the notice board, turn right and walk along the lane away from Bloxholm Hall and its surrounding woods. After bending right the lane bends left, and here the walk keeps straight ahead along the farm drive. Where the track curves left, towards Hill Farm, go keep ahead on a public footpath through the trees. It's a clear and direct route that keeps just inside the southern edge of Spruce Covert and, after eventually swinging right, it then bears left to leave the main wood and follow the middle of a wide strip of trees, known as the Long Plantation.

The woods are rich in birdlife, although to identify them you will have to use your ears as well as your eyes. The "pink, pink" is likely to be a chaffinch, while the great tit's distinctive call sounds like "teacher, teacher", plus a metallic series of "zee-de" notes. Another common woodland bird, which arrives from late March onwards, is the chiffchaff. Its loud and plaintive "hoo-eet" is often followed by a monotonous

### WHAT TO LOOK FOR

The elegant spire of St Hybald's at Ashby de la Launde will be a familiar landmark on this walk. Hidden away in the woodland surrounding the former hall is Bloxholm Church. The parish church of Dorrington has no spire or tower at all.

# BLOXHOLM

"chiff-chaff, chiff-chaff". Out on the open farmland and by the hedgerows listen out for the yellowhammer's high-pitched "little bit of bread and no cheese".

Since the path skirts the edge of the wood there are occasional views out across the open farmland, which to the south includes the site of the deserted medieval village of Brauncewell. A scattering of low, rectangular earthworks is all that remains of up to 25 buildings, while around the church, rebuilt in 1855, is the outline of what were thought to be once the grand gardens of the Manor House. If you look on the Ordnance Survey map you will see that another lost village, Dunsby, is located less than a mile (1.6km) away by the present-day A15. Across the country there are many more examples of villages simply wiped out during the Middle Ages, and more than 235 have been identified in Lincolnshire alone. It's commonly thought that the Black Death, which arrived in England in 1348, was the main culprit, but in fact it was more likely owing to failed harvests and famine, and in particular the clearance of whole communities to make way for sheep grazing. For a close-up view of the Brauncewell site take the path across the fields towards Manor Farm that leaves the Bloxholm lane 0.5 mile (800m) south of the Stepping Out car park.

When you reach a junction of paths turn right, past a reedy pond, and follow this permissive route up towards Mount Farm. At the lane at the top turn right and walk along this wide, hedged track eastwards for about a mile (1.6km), passing through several farm gates. The distant church spire and distinctive water tower seen away to the left belong to the village of Ashby de la Launde. Ashby, which means 'settlement by the ash trees', is quite a common name in Lincolnshire and Leicestershire, but to distinguish itself Ashby de la Launde (like Ashby de la Zouche, near Leicester) has retained the name of its Norman landlord.

The dead-straight track continues over a wooded rise, known as The Mount, then descends to continue through two fields, separated by a gate and stile, towards the former Bloxholm Hall. The original house was built in the 1600s but, despite subsequent enlargement, most of it was pulled down three centuries later.

At the perimeter fence turn right and walk alongside this to the corner of the field. Here go straight on, through a small but obvious gap in the thin line of trees, and turn left. With fields on your right, and some houses and a long red-brick wall on your left, walk as far as the road and turn right to return to the car park.

# The Wildlife of Daneshill Lakes

**WALK 11**

*A very easy stroll around a watery nature reserve, reclaimed from old gravel pits near Retford in north Nottinghamshire.*

---

**DISTANCE** 3 miles (4.8km)  **MINIMUM TIME** 1hr 30min

**ASCENT/GRADIENT** Negligible ▲▲▲  **LEVEL OF DIFFICULTY** ✚✚✚

**PATHS** Firm gravel tracks and woodland paths

**LANDSCAPE** Small lakes and pools dotted around mixed woodland

**SUGGESTED MAP** OS Explorer 279 Doncaster

**START/FINISH** Grid reference: SK 668865

**DOG FRIENDLINESS** On lead, except in designated 'dog run' area

**PARKING** Nature reserve car park, Daneshill Road, signed from A638

**PUBLIC TOILETS** None on route (nearest in Retford)

---

Daneshill Lakes Local Nature Reserve was created in the mid-1980s from a collection of shallow gravel extraction pits as part of a major reclamation project by Nottinghamshire County Council. It falls into two distinct parts, separated by Daneshill Road. To the south, leading off from the car park, is the more open and popular section, with benches and picnic tables, where windsurfers ply the main lake and anglers sit patiently by the shore. Coots and moorhens busy themselves among the reeds, and Canada geese, grebes and swans are a common sight. Across the road to the north is a more wooded and secluded area that is specially managed for wildlife. Walkers are likely to spot plenty of birds, such as goldcrests and coal tits, and even the odd sparrowhawk shooting out of the trees at great speed. This is certainly the place to make sure you have your binoculars and identification book handy.

Despite being close to the road and a mainline railway, Daneshill Lakes provide a wonderful oasis for birdlife, partly because of the variety of different habitats – from open water and wetland through to scrub and woodland – so that you are almost as likely to see waders such as redshank and ringed plover as you are wood warblers, blackcaps and any of the three native British woodpeckers. But there is much else besides the birds, since dragonflies and damselflies take to the air when the summer temperatures rise sufficiently, and newts and toads revel in the wet and sheltered thickets.

## Star Millennium Pathway

This innovative route, which encompasses Daneshill Lakes, was designed as part of the local millennium celebrations and links the nearby villages of Scrooby, Ranskill and Torworth. All three of the settlements are connected by the Great North Road (which used to be part of the A1, but is now reduced in status to the A638) as well as the railway, and historically have always shared schools, churches and other adminstrative aspects. The 'Star' is the name of the local newsletter which is produced and distributed among the villages.

# DANESHILL LAKES

## The Pilgrim Fathers Heritage

Today the small village of Scrooby (3 miles/4.8km north of Daneshill Lakes) seems a very quiet and unassuming sort of place, but its significance in history is confirmed by the name of the pub – The Pilgrim Fathers.

Local man William Brewster, who lived at the manor house, rebelled against the orthodox Church by actively promoting what was called Separatism. But early 17th-century England wasn't exactly tolerant of religious dissenters, and Brewster ended up fleeing to Holland. In the autumn of 1620 he set sail for North America on board the *Mayflower*, with the other so-called Pilgrim Fathers, to head west to start a new life. The rest, as they say, is history.

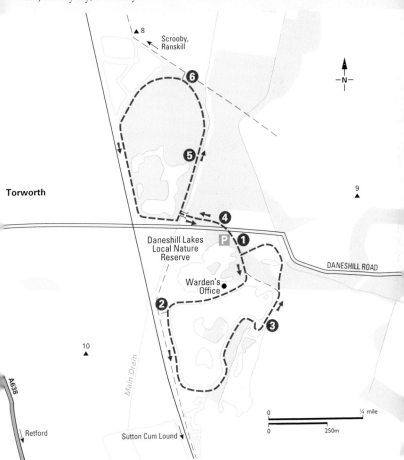

## WALK 11 DIRECTIONS

❶ From the car park go through the main gate and ahead past the notice board on the wide gravel track. At the junction swing right, so that the large lake opens up on your left. Go past the warden's office and sailing club hut along the water's edge.

❷ Approaching the railway look for the two large track-side signs which read 'Edinburgh 250 miles'. (Fortunately today's walk is a little less ambitious.) The first left turn is a continuation of the lakeside path, and the second left is via the dog-run next to the railway. Both join up 350yds (320m) later and resume the easy tour around the main lake. A second, smaller lake opens up on the right.

❸ When you meet the fence at the end, with an open field beyond, turn left. As this bears left after 300yds (274m) take the small grassy path into the woods half right, beside a notice board about the former Ranskill Royal Ordnance Factory on this site. You now follow a millennium wildlife trail indicated by wooden posts bearing the letters 'MM'. It wanders happily through the bushes and trees and beside a small stream (look out for the pond-dipping platform), and when it finally emerges from the undergrowth turn right to return to the car park. Continue via the small path through the trees to the left of the road entrance and cross the road.

### WHERE TO EAT AND DRINK

Refreshments are to be found at local pubs, such as The Pilgrim Fathers at Scrooby, Blue Bell at Ranskill and The Huntsman at Torworth, plus there's the Village Fish Bar at Ranskill. Another option is to take an easy public footpath from the southern edge of the reserve across the fields to visit The Gate Inn at Sutton Cum Lound, a round trip of just over 2 miles (3.2km).

❹ Go through the gateway on the opposite side and turn left on to a narrow path, indicated 'Easy Access to Reserve' (ignore the wide grassy footpath to the right). Follow this track until you reach a wooden footbridge. Go across, then turn right and walk along to reach the notice board by the woodland pond.

### WHILE YOU'RE THERE

The market town of Retford, 4 miles (6.4km) south of Daneshill Lakes, retains a number of attractive Georgian and Victorian buildings, many bordering the elegant Market Square. Leading off from this is Grove Street where, situated next to the tourist information centre, is Bassetlaw Museum, which has more details on the town's history and the area's historic connection with the English Puritan movement that went on to found America.

❺ Continue to follow this easy and obvious track through the reserve, keeping the ditch and stream on your right-hand side and ignoring an inviting turning to the right across a footbridge.

❻ Unless you want to make a diversion at this point to visit Ranskill as well, ignore the right turn for the Millennium Pathway, and instead stick to the main path as it completes a giant loop around the entire nature reserve. Look out for the shallow pools and scrapes among the undergrowth, which, unless they've dried out in hot weather, are a focus for creatures such as frogs and beetles. After about a mile (1.6km) or so you arrive back at the wooden footbridge. Turn right here to cross it, go through the gateway to the road and cross over to the car park.

### WHAT TO LOOK FOR

If you visit in the spring or summer, look out for butterflies, such as the meadow brown, the common blue and the dull-orange/brown gatekeeper – all attracted by the brambles and gorse. The bright yellow of the male brimstone is striking, and as it overwinters as an adult it is often the first butterfly to appear on the wing in spring.

# Enjoying Country Life at Clumber

*Nottinghamshire's Clumber Park provides an undemanding and enjoyable day out for all ages.*

WALK 12

---

**DISTANCE** 3.75 miles (6km)   **MINIMUM TIME** 1hr 30min

**ASCENT/GRADIENT** 131ft (40m) ▲▲▲   **LEVEL OF DIFFICULTY** ✦✦✦

**PATHS** Clear, level paths and tracks throughout, some steps

**LANDSCAPE** Landscaped parkland surrounding ornamental lake

**SUGGESTED MAP** OS Explorer 270 Sherwood Forest

**START/FINISH** Grid reference: SK 625745

**DOG FRIENDLINESS** Generally good, with off-lead areas

**PARKING** Main car park in Clumber Park (pay-and-display)

**PUBLIC TOILETS** At car park, and half-way round near Hardwick village

---

There are few more popular and scenic locations for a family day out in the East Midlands than Clumber Park, with walking and cycling routes aplenty. What is rather bizarre, however, is that the centrepiece of the original estate vanished many years ago.

The building of Clumber House didn't begin until the 18th century but, typical of the age, the Duke of Newcastle, who had been granted the right to enclose what was until then a part of Sherwood Forest, set about it in style. Gatehouses and follies sprang up, and the River Poulter was dammed to form a vast lake complete with boathouses and a classical bridge (although, it took 15 years and over £6,000 to build). A small chain ferry was installed to cross the lake, and a full-time sailor was even employed to crew a model naval frigate called *The Lincoln*, which resided on the water as a floating summer house until it caught fire and sank in the 1940s. The house was filled with rare books and paintings, while the park was planted with thousands of trees, including a 2-mile (3.2km) avenue of limes which, it is claimed, remains the longest in Europe.

However, after the death of the 7th Duke of Newcastle in 1928 the fortune of Clumber took a turn for the worse, and the exorbitant running costs of the huge house and estate forced its closure. The contents of the house were sold off at auction and the redundant building was demolished ten years later. During the Second World War the park was requisitioned for trials of new military equipment, and on one occasion Winston Churchill visited to view a new trench-digging machine known as the 'White Rabbit' (the scars on the land can still be seen).

## Clumber Saved for the Nation

Happily for Clumber, the National Trust stepped in and negotiated to purchase the 3,800-acre (1,539ha) park as part of its Golden Jubilee celebrations in 1945. The land includes extensive tracts of grassland and heathland, in addition to the formal walkways and avenues. However, almost half of Clumber Park is taken up by woodland, with a wonderful array of mature beech, oak, chestnut and pine, as well as more exotic introductions.

41

# CLUMBER PARK

A tree nursery is also being developed to grow trees from seed collected in the park, and among the other visitor attractions is a walled kitchen garden, which apart from organically managed vegetable plots also features a palm house, vines and figs.

Although the house is long gone, the original stable blocks now serves as the information point, with adjacent tea rooms, and near by the Clumber Chapel, begun in 1868 and a wonderful example of extravagant Gothic Revival architecture, is still used three Sundays a month for services.

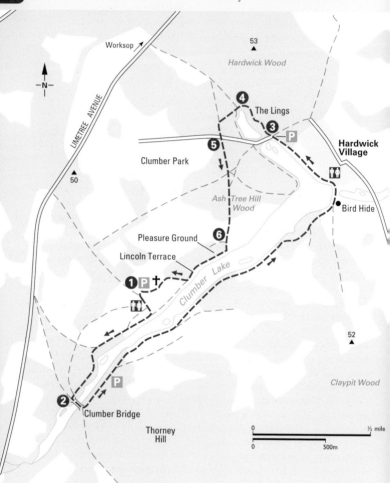

## WALK 12 DIRECTIONS

❶ From the information point near the main car park, walk across the site of the former mansion and down to reach the lakeside. Turn right here along the clear path that runs along the shore through an area of patchy

woodland. Continue to follow the path, which curves left, then right, all the way to Clumber Bridge.

❷ Cross the bridge and turn left past the car park to resume the route by the shore. If the path by the water's edge below the trees is a little boggy, then switch to the wider and firmer track further back. As you draw opposite the site of the former house, there are paths off across the parkland to your right – a detailed map is available from the National Trust shop. At the far corner of the lake you eventually swing left on the embankment path. To your right you'll find an area of wetland created 20 years ago by mining subsidence, now a popular area for birding. Carry on past the toilet block at Hardwick until you reach the surfaced road beyond the car park.

### WHERE TO EAT AND DRINK

The National Trust restaurant at Clumber Park serves excellent home-cooked food, with an emphasis on locally sourced meat plus vegetables and herbs from the walled kitchen garden. There is also a snack kiosk at busy times. It goes without saying that Clumber Park is a great place to bring a picnic, and there is even a designated barbecue area to the north of the park off Limetree Avenue.

❸ Go left on to the road and in 50yds (46m) turn right, before the causeway begins, for a narrow, sandy path up through dense vegetation. Follow this twisting route through an area known as The Lings. The huge variety of

### WHAT TO LOOK FOR

Although some of Clumber's oldest woodland dates from the 1500s, most of the mature oak, pines, chestnut and beech you see today were planted two centuries later. The formal avenues of lime, cedar and beech followed afterwards, while most of the larch and pine plantations that dot the perimeter of the park are relatively recent additions.

trees here includes beech, sweet chestnut, silver birch, yew and pines. When you drop down and emerge into an open, flat area beyond the end of the lake, walk ahead to turn left on to a wide, curving gravel track.

❹ In a few paces, where this narrowing route veers left towards the shore, go straight on along the left of two grassy paths. At the end turn left on to a wide track that crosses the road and continues past a wooden barrier into Ash Tree Hill Wood.

❺ Go straight over a crossroads of tracks and on along this popular and direct route through the trees, ignoring an inviting right turn. When you emerge in open ground on the far side, continue ahead to the ornate gateway into the wooded Pleasure Ground ahead.

### WHILE YOU'RE THERE

In contrast to the lavish acres of Clumber Park, the National Trust's 300 historic houses also include smaller properties such as Mr Straw's House, a semi-detached Edwardian house in nearby Worksop which is almost totally unaltered since the 1930s. Complete with period furniture, costumes and memorabilia, it's located at 7 Blyth Grove and is open Tuesday to Saturday, April to October (advance booking only).

❻ Go through this, and veer left on any one of the minor paths through the undergrowth to reach the main lakeside route. Turn right and follow this along Lincoln Terrace back to the start of the walk. A little beyond the lawned terrace a looping track to the right, across the carefully manicured lawns, leads you to the chapel and car park.

# A Merrie Tale
# of Sherwood Forest

*Enjoy a fascinating and enchanting walk among
the age-old oaks of this legendary forest.*

---

**DISTANCE** *5.5 miles (8.8km)* **MINIMUM TIME** *2hrs 30min*

**ASCENT/GRADIENT** *278ft (85m)* ▲▲▲ **LEVEL OF DIFFICULTY** ✦✦✦

**PATHS** *Easy woodland tracks and wide forest rides*

**LANDSCAPE** *Beautiful mixed woodland, more open to north*

**SUGGESTED MAP** *OS Explorer 270 Sherwood Forest*

**START/FINISH** *Grid reference: SK 626676*

**DOG FRIENDLINESS** *On lead around Visitor Centre, otherwise excellent*

**PARKING** *Sherwood Forest Visitor Centre (pay-and-display)*

**PUBLIC TOILETS** *Sherwood Forest Visitor Centre*

---

If Robin Hood or one of his merrie men were to return to Sherwood Forest today they would no doubt be surprised at how dramatically it has shrunk. The modern Sherwood Forest Country Park covers 450 acres (182ha), whereas the original area was more like 100,000 acres (40,500ha). But there again this vast ancient forest, which at the time of the Norman Conquest covered most of Nottinghamshire north of the River Trent, was not in fact a blanket forest but a mix of wood, heathland and scrub. It was the preserve of the nobility, where the King and his entourage hunted deer, and the commoners were subject to strict Forest Laws that could see a man's hand cut off for poaching.

## Mighty Oaks from Little Acorns Grow

In England and Wales 'ancient woodland' generally refers to woods that have existed since 1600 (1750 in Scotland). Here at Sherwood the surviving woodland, though small, is a wonderful mix of native broadleaved varieties, dominated by oak and birch. Both varieties of native British oak can be found in the forest – common or English oak, and sessile or durmast oak – while newer conifer plantations extend the tree cover east and west.

The ancient woodland is full of light and atmosphere, and makes for magical walking. The highlight, however, is the gigantic old oak trees that pepper the forest. There are more than 900 trees above 600 years old (sometimes known as 'druids'), and while a few are simply gnarled and hollow old stumps, others still dominate the surroundings with their massive 'stag heads' of twisted limbs and spreading foliage.

The most famous of these is the Major Oak, visited on this walk, and one of the largest trees in England. Its exact age is somewhat uncertain, estimates having varied over the years from 500–1,500 years, but there's no doubting its sheer size. The hollow trunk is 33ft (10m) in circumference, and such is the spread of its colossal branches (92ft/28m) that they have to be propped up with artificial supports. But whether even the Major Oak's hollow trunk could have hidden Robin Hood and his entire band of merrie men, as legend has it, is rather more doubtful.

# SHERWOOD FOREST

## A Changing Landscape

Sherwood Forest has changed from a royal hunting ground to a source of valuable raw material. The use of English oak by everyone from shipbuilders and furniture-makers to miners and charcoal burners mean that between 1609 and 1790 their number plummeted by 80 per cent.

In 2005, Sherwood Forest was declared a National Nature Reserve, and there are plans to move the Visitor Centre to a new location outside the boundary of the reserve. It is expected to open in 2010 on the site of the former Thoresby Colliery, just east of the B6034 at Edwinstowe.

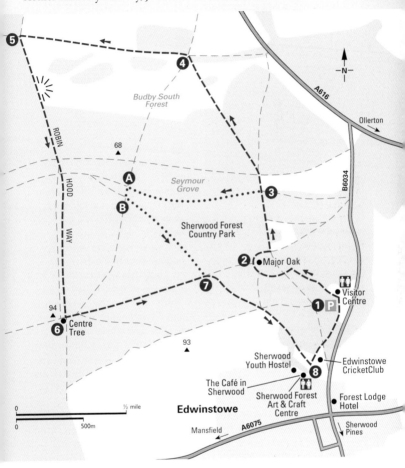

## WALK 13 DIRECTIONS

❶ Facing the main entrance to Sherwood Forest Visitor Centre from the car park, turn left and follow the well-signposted route to the Major Oak.

❷ Go along the curving path as it completes a semi-circle around the impressive old tree and continue as far as the junction with a public bridleway (signposted). Turn left here, then walk this straight and uncomplicated route for 0.25 mile (400m), ignoring all paths off.

❸ At a green notice board, warning of a nearby military

training area, the main path bears left. Instead go straight ahead, past the metal bar gate, for a path that continues over a crossroads to become a wide, fenced track through pleasant open country of heather and bracken known as Budby South Forest.

❹ At the very far side go through a gate and turn left on to an unmade lane, and walk this undulating route for 0.75 mile (1.2km).

---

### WHILE YOU'RE THERE

A few miles to the south of the country park, off the B6030 by Clipstone, is Sherwood Pines Forest Park. This huge Forestry Commission plantation incorporates a variety of waymarked trails for walkers and cyclists, and offers a bike-hire service for all the family.

---

❺ At the major junction just before the plantation begins, turn left, indicated 'Centre Tree'. With the rows of conifers on your right, and good views across Budby South Forest on your left, keep to this straight and obvious track. Where the track divides into two parallel trails, the gravelly track on the right is technically the cycle route, while the more leafy and grassy ride to the left is the bridleway, but either can be used.

❻ When you reach the Centre Tree – a huge spreading oak – the two routes converge to continue past a bench down a wide avenue among the trees.

---

### WHERE TO EAT AND DRINK

The Forest Table Restaurant at Sherwood Forest Visitor Centre is open daily for hot meals and snacks. The Café in Sherwood Forest, at Sherwood Forest Art & Craft Centre, serves lunches, cream teas and home-made cakes from Tuesday to Sunday in summer and Wednesday to Sunday in winter. For a wider range of food, there are pubs and restaurants in Edwinstowe.

---

Don't go down this, but instead turn left and, ignoring paths off right and left, carry straight on along the main track back into the heart of the forest.

❼ After almost 0.75 mile (1.2km) you pass a metal bar gate on the right and then meet a bridleway coming in from the left. Ignoring the inviting path straight ahead (which returns to the Major Oak) bear right on the main track, past some bare holes and dips hollowed out by children's bikes. At a large junction of criss-crossing routes go straight on (signposted 'Fairground') so that an open field and distant housing becomes visible to your right. This wide sandy track descends to a field by Edwinstowe cricket ground. The Art and Craft Centre and Sherwood Youth Hostel are on the far side, and the village centre beyond.

❽ To return to the visitor centre and car park, follow the well-walked, signposted track back up past the cricket ground.

---

### WHAT TO LOOK FOR

Part of the ongoing attraction of ancient oak woodlands, such as Sherwood Forest, is that they encourage a healthy wildlife count. Oak trees, for instance, support the greatest number of fungi of any native tree, and as many as 1,500 species of beetle can be found. Warblers and woodpeckers are joined by more unusual birds such as the nightjar. The hollow interior of the grand old oaks are particularly valuable (signs ask children not to clamber over them), providing a place of hibernation for bats, butterflies and spiders.

---

# A Shorter Sherwood Forest Walk

*This easier option is ideal for those after the gentlest of strolls.*
**See map and information panel for Walk 13**

---

**DISTANCE** 3.25 miles (5.3km)   **MINIMUM TIME** 1hr 30min
**ASCENT/GRADIENT** 164ft (50m) ▲▲▲   **LEVEL OF DIFFICULTY** ✚✚✚

---

## WALK 14 DIRECTIONS
### (Walk 13 option)

At Point ❸ follow the main track as it bends left by the green notice board entitled 'Dukeries Training Area' and carry on along this wide and obvious route. To the right is Seymour Grove, a coniferous plantation that is in stark contrast to the more mixed and attractive oak woodland to your left. Look out for several old oak trunks, hollow and slowly rotting, but still awesome in their size. How old do you think they are? One of the problems with accurately ageing the Major Oak is that experts believe that over the centuries several different oak trees may have fused into the one main specimen that is seen today.

After roughly 0.6 mile (1.1km) turn left on to a clear public footpath (Point ❹), then in a few paces branch left again on a short linking path to join a major bridleway leftwards (Point ❺). If you accidentally over-shoot the first turning you will meet the signposted bridleway 300yds (274m) further up the path, and so turn sharp left here and follow this route back and stay on it.

The bridleway heads south eastwards through the heart of the forest, via open glades and groves of silver birch. Little paths

disappear off into the trees, and it is easy to imagine a small band of outlaws vanishing into the woodland without a trace. In medieval times the forest would almost certainly have played host to such gangs, but whether they were led by Robin of Locksley is another matter.

After a little under 0.5 mile (800m) you reach a junction of tracks (Point ❼). From here continue straight on to resume the main route, or turn left for a short path back to the Major Oak and the visitor centre beyond.

### WHAT TO LOOK FOR

The annual Robin Hood Festival takes place during the school summer holidays, when the Visitor Centre puts on a variety of themed events – from archery and jousting to falconry and entertainers. If you want to learn more about life in a medieval forest, the exhibitions at the Visitor Centre include the Spirit of Sherwood film show, Robyn Hode's Sherwode and Sherwood Past, Present and Future.

# Ministering the Flock

*An exploration of historic Southwell,*
*from lofty towers to famous apples.*

WALK 15

---

DISTANCE 4.25 miles (6.8km)   MINIMUM TIME 2hrs

ASCENT/GRADIENT 246ft (75m) ▲▲▲   LEVEL OF DIFFICULTY +++

PATHS Easy tracks and field paths, riverside path, 1 stile

LANDSCAPE Small, quiet town surrounded by gentle farmland

SUGGESTED MAP OS Explorers 270 Sherwood Forest; 271 Newark

START/FINISH Grid reference: SK 701539 (on Explorer 271)

DOG FRIENDLINESS Generally very good, but remember to scoop poop

PARKING Car park opposite minster on Church Street (free for first two hours)

PUBLIC TOILETS By car park

---

## WALK 15 DIRECTIONS

The small Nottinghamshire market town of Southwell is dominated by the 12th-century minster, which was technically elevated to the status of a cathedral when the new Diocese of Southwell was created in 1884. Make sure you set aside some time to explore this spacious and splendid building which has a fine example of a Norman nave, plus a chapter house containing intricate 13th-century carvings of leaves, which were supposedly modelled on trees from the old Sherwood Forest. Outside are the ruins of an earlier archbishops' palace, while the two distinctive conical towers make the minster a recognisable landmark from several points on the walk.

From the car park, facing the minster, turn right on to Church Street and walk up to the junction at the top. In a 16th-century inn opposite, originally called the King's Head, Charles I spent his last hours of freedom before surrendering to the Scottish army which was at Newark Castle. The inn's name was changed to the Saracens Head when Charles was beheaded.

Turn right, then cross the road and turn left into Queen Street. Follow this for 350yds (320m), then turn left on to a short drive, opposite a road called The Ropewalk. At the end, continue uphill on an alleyway by a school, and at the far corner turn right along the top of the playing field. At a junction of paths go forwards, down a few steps, and on along a path behind gardens. Eventually you cross a road and continue on the far side on a field-edge path on the far side. Where this approaches the bend of a road turn sharply right

### WHAT TO LOOK FOR

On the streets adjoining the Minster are a number of highly elegant mansions known as Prebendal Houses. These were the town homes of the 16 secular canons who originally formed the Chapter of the Collegiate Church, and who were collectively called Prebendaries because they received incomes from endowed estates.

for a short path across the field. Cross the road at the far side and go through a gap in the hedge to pick up a broad track past a fruit farm (masses of strawberries are a common sight here) and an orchard on the right.

Another of Southwell's claims to fame involves the humble apple. According to the story, nurseryman Henry Merryweather took a cutting from a new and unusual apple tree in the garden of a cottage in Church Street belonging to a Matthew Bramley, some time around 1850. The propagation proved successful and the classic English cooking apple has never looked back. It's celebrated locally in the Southwell Galette, a delectable pastry confection of sultanas, hazelnuts and Bramley apples.

Continue straight ahead through the orchards until you reach a junction of paved lanes. To the left is a rather grand-looking house, while to the right is a small fishing lake. This is all part of Norwood Park, the last surviving of four elegant parks created around Southwell for the Archbishop of York, since Southwell was originally one of three collegiate churches in the huge York Diocese (the others were Beverley and Ripon).

Keep straight ahead past the golf course on your right. At the road at the end turn right, then turn left almost immediately on to a lane indicated 'Maythorne'. After a couple of bends the lane is crossed by the former Mansfield –Southwell railway line, which has been turned into a pleasant walking and cycling route known as the Southwell Trail.

For a quicker and easier return to Southwell, turn right and follow its unswerving course for just under 1 mile (1.6km) to the car park at the end. Otherwise continue to the far end of the lane and go through the former mill buildings in order to turn left, across the bridge, and then veer right at a choice of paths. Go over a short footbridge and stile, and turn right for a riverside path along the River Greet (this is also the route of the waymarked Robin Hood Way).

After just over a mile (1.6km) you reach another converted mill building. Turn right on to Station Road and walk up past the Southwell Trail car park and The Newcastle Arms pub to the crossroads. Go over this and walk across the tree-lined Burgage Green. On the right is an intimidating stone gatehouse complete with iron grid bars, all that remains of a 19th-century 'House of Correction'. At the war memorial at the far end take the side road half left, and at the end of this turn left on to Burgage Lane. Just before Hill House turn right on to a narrow alleyway called Becher's Walk which will take you all the way down to Church Street. Turn right for the minster and car park.

# Byron's Romantic Home

*Explore a beautiful Nottinghamshire mansion south of Mansfield, that was once home to the English Romantic poet Byron.*

**WALK 16**

---

**DISTANCE** 5.75 miles (9.2km)   **MINIMUM TIME** 2hrs 30min

**ASCENT/GRADIENT** 460ft (140m) ▲▲▲   **LEVEL OF DIFFICULTY** ✦✦✦

**PATHS** Firm, uncomplicated paths and tracks, 1 stile

**LANDSCAPE** Parkland, woodland and villages

**SUGGESTED MAP** OS Explorer 270 Sherwood Forest

**START/FINISH** Grid reference: SK 541540

**DOG FRIENDLINESS** Good, but under close control in grounds and gardens

**PARKING** Newstead Abbey car park, access from A60 (note closing times)

**PUBLIC TOILETS** At Newstead Abbey

---

Newstead Abbey was established by Henry II in the late 12th century, supposedly in atonement for the murder of Thomas à Becket at Canterbury, and the elegant remains of the priory church alone would be reason enough to visit today. However, in 1540 Newstead was handed over to the Byron family by another King Henry not so enamoured by the pious monks, and 250 years later it came into the possession of George Gordon, the 6th Lord Byron and celebrated English Romantic poet.

### Mad, Bad and Dangerous to Know

The Newstead that Byron inherited was empty and dilapidated, thanks to the profligate 5th Lord who had run up huge debts, so he furnished just a few rooms and used the empty ones to indulge his passion for boxing, fencing and pistol shooting, and letting his animals run wild (including dogs, tortoises, and at one stage even a bear!).

The restless young man had a string of tempestuous relationships, and in 1816 moved to Italy to travel Europe in search of love, freedom and inspiration for his poetry. He was a great champion of liberty and throwing off the shackles of tyranny, once writing an impassioned piece about the treatment of English factory workers, and his final year was spent in Greece leading local freedom fighters. Byron's work continues to be read and quoted to this day – during the Solidarity strike in Poland in the 1980s and by the protesting students at Tiananmen Square in China a decade later.

When Byron disposed of Newstead Abbey in 1817 it passed through several different owners before being presented to Nottingham Corporation in 1931. Today its grand rooms, halls and libraries are open to the public between April and September, and there are fascinating displays which give an informative insight into the illustrious Byron family, including letters, furniture and other possessions that belonged to the poet. In addition to the later Victorian furnishings there are period costumes and also reproduction clothes which you are invited to try on.

Behind the house is a spread of lakes, lawns and formal gardens (from a Japanese garden through to the monks' garden and rose garden), plus a picnic area and children's playground. In all the park extends for 300 acres (121ha) and is open all year round.

Allow at least an hour to do justice to the house, and the same again to walk around the beautiful gardens. It is important to note that the car park is locked at 6pm in summer and 4pm in winter. If you do not plan to visit the house and gardens, it may be better to park free of charge in Linby and start the walk from there.

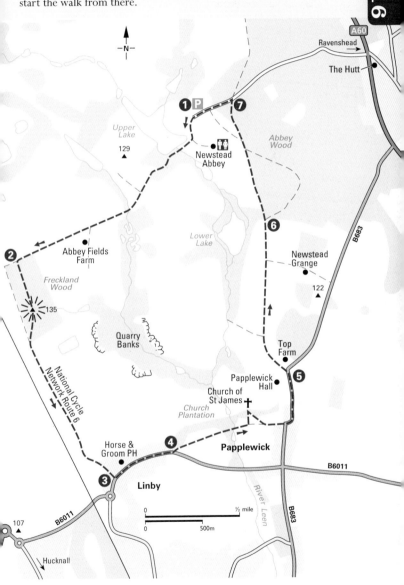

## WALK 16 DIRECTIONS

❶ From the main car park walk down the drive the short distance to the abbey, then on along the tarmac lane below the large Upper Lake. Follow this easy route for 1.25 miles (2km) until you leave

# NEWSTEAD ABBEY

the perimeter of the park after the second lodge.

**2** Immediately turn left and cross the stile to reach a small, dumpy hill adorned with young trees (Freckland Wood). An airy and quite easy path runs up and across its panoramic top, or else you can skirt its right-hand foot on the waymarked National Cycle Network Route 6. Both routes meet up on the far corner for a direct 1.25-mile (2km) track all the way to Linby.

**3** Turn left when you emerge close to the roundabout, and walk along the pavement through the village as far as the Horse & Groom pub. Cross over to inspect the notice board by the bus stop detailing the village's history, then continue eastwards out of the village on the pavement opposite the second of two medieval road-side crosses.

**4** When the left-hand pavement ends cross over once more and take a popular local footpath across Church Plantation. Continue across the River Leen, then halfway up the next field go through the archway in the hedge on the left to reach the tiny Church of St James. Leave the churchyard, via the main gate, and proceed down the surfaced drive to the main road. Turn left and walk along the pavement for 550yds (503m) until the entrance for Papplewick Hall.

**5** Turn left, not to enter the hall's gated driveway but for the wide, semi-surfaced Hall Lane that runs via a green gate past Top Farm. Where the lane bends sharply left, around a prominent brick wall, go straight on, via a gate, along the hedged farm track across the fields. Where the farm track turns right to Newstead Grange, go straight on along the main grassy track towards the wooded perimeter of the park.

**6** Follow the waymarks around the lodge and continue along a surfaced drive through the trees – look out for some ancient beech and oak along the way. About 0.75 mile (1.2km) beyond the lodge, the lane bends left and the path branches off ahead/right, clearly indicated. Soon it drops down to reach the main drive to the abbey.

**7** Turn left and walk along the road to the car park and abbey for some well-earned refreshments, and perhaps a spot of poetry.

# In the Footsteps of D H Lawrence at Eastwood

*Explore the countryside around the Nottinghamshire town that provided inspiration for much of the writer's work.*

---

**DISTANCE** 5.75 miles (9.2km)  **MINIMUM TIME** 2hrs 30min

**ASCENT/GRADIENT** 360ft (110m) ▲▲▲  **LEVEL OF DIFFICULTY** ✦✦✦

**PATHS** Rough field and woodland tracks, 2 stiles

**LANDSCAPE** Farmland and woods, red-brick towns and villages

**SUGGESTED MAP** OS Explorer 260 Nottingham

**START/FINISH** Grid reference: SK 481481

**DOG FRIENDLINESS** On lead at start (poop scoop by-laws apply)

**PARKING** Colliers Wood car park, Engine Lane, off B600

**PUBLIC TOILETS** None on route (nearest in Eastwood)

---

David Herbert Lawrence was one of the most commanding English writers of the early 20th century, but his Nottinghamshire roots were distinctly humble. He came from the industrial town of Eastwood, north-west of Nottingham, and the terrace house he was born in has been preserved as a museum. Although his father was a miner, the boy's academic expertise won him a scholarship to Nottingham High School and, after a short spell teaching in south London, he concentrated on writing full-time.

## Eastwood in Print

Lawrence's intense feeling for what he called 'the country of my heart' manifested itself in his writing, and many of the places you will see on this walk are represented in his books and short stories. Greasley Church is Minton in *Sons and Lovers*, and Felley Mill is turned into Strelley Mill in *The White Peacock*, his first novel. Some had dark associations, such as Moorgreen Reservoir which as Willey Water in *Women in Love* (and Nethermere in *Sons and Lovers*) was the scene of a drowning tragedy – based, in fact, on a real incident. All the way around this walk, which forms part of a local heritage trail, there are well-designed boards relating the landscape to the stories.

But his depiction of Eastwood as a dour little mining town was often unflattering and caused so much local resentment that his name was hardly mentioned for some years. Mind you, his books often had troubled lives of their own. His novel *The Rainbow* was at first banned for alleged obscenity, and the full publication of his most notorious book, *Lady Chatterley's Lover*, was delayed for over 30 years and led to a celebrated court case concerning its supposedly graphic sex scenes.

The walk begins at the site of the former Moorgreen Colliery, renamed Minton Pit by Lawrence in *Sons and Lovers*. Moorgreen was producing more than one million tons of coal a year as recently as the 1960s, but the seams were eventually exhausted and in 1985 the colliery closed. After landscaping the site was renamed Colliers Wood, and as part of Nottinghamshire's Greenwood Community Forest it has been planted with shrubs and trees, and ponds and wetland have been established to attract wildlife.

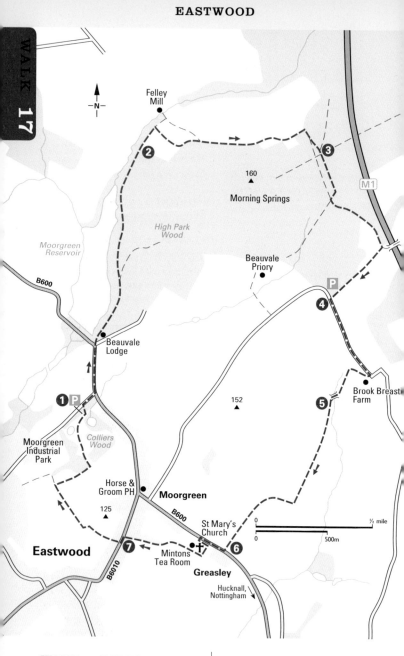

## WALK 17 DIRECTIONS

**❶** Walk out of the entrance of Colliers Wood car park and turn right, then left along the pavement of the B600. At the bend turn right by Beauvale Lodge and take the track to its left (signposted

'Felley Mill'). Walk this pleasant fenced route through High Park Wood, above Moorgreen Reservoir, branching left after 0.25 mile (400m) just before a gate. Carry on along the main track until an open field appears on your right.

WALK 17

❷ Continue walking for another 150yds (137m), then turn right at the stile and walk up the left-hand side of a patchy line of trees separating two fields. At the far side turn left and follow the woodland edge. Go around the corner and, joining a wide farm track, continue alongside the forest. (The site of Felley Mill is away to your left at the foot of the slope.) After 0.5 mile (800m) turn right beyond the bench to locate a public footpath through the trees.

❸ Where this emerges at a junction of three forest rides go straight ahead. With the growl of the nearby M1 motorway getting louder, turn left after the bend on to a clearly indicated footpath into the woods. This emerges to follow the edge of a field, swinging right on the far side and eventually reaching a lay-by.

❹ Turn right if you want to view the remains of Beauvale Priory, otherwise go left and walk down the lane to the bend by the intriguingly named 'Brook Breasting Farm'. Go sharply right, along the left-hand edge of a field, then turn left and drop down through two more fields. Look for the gap in the undergrowth to the right, and go over a footbridge.

❺ Turn left and follow the direction of the sign across the lower part of the field. Continue along the top edge of successive fields, going right to skirt the final sloping field before dropping down to the road.

❻ Cross over and turn right to enter the churchyard of St Mary's at Greasley. Walk around the church and exit the churchyard at the far side on a footpath signposted 'Moorgreen'. After crossing the cemetery, go across the field and continue to walk alongside paddocks to reach the road at the top.

❼ Turn left and almost immediately right for an enclosed path between houses. Follow the waymarks across and down through fields, and at the bottom go right for the path back into Colliers Wood. Turn first left to reach the ponds, and beyond is the car park.

# Deep in the Dumbles

*The hidden dells of Lambley's Dumbles*
*make Nottingham seem far away.*

DISTANCE *6.25 miles (10.1km)*   MINIMUM TIME *3hrs*

ASCENT/GRADIENT *508ft (155m)* ▲▲▲   LEVEL OF DIFFICULTY +++

PATHS *Undulating paths and green lanes, over 20 stiles*

LANDSCAPE *Rolling farmland, pockets of woodland and villages*

SUGGESTED MAP *OS Explorer 260 Nottingham*

START/FINISH *Grid reference: SK 627452*

DOG FRIENDLINESS *Close supervision around livestock, note stiles*

PARKING *Recreation ground car park behind school (opposite The Lambley, on Catfoot Lane)*

PUBLIC TOILETS *Floralands Garden Village, I mile (1.6km) up Catfoot Lane*

Dumble is a local term for a small wooded dell through which streams have carved out twisting and steep-sided gullies. The main one is simply called Lambley Dumble, and is visited at the end of this walk. From a distance the snaking line of trees and bushes looks like a narrow copse or old field boundary, but often they disguise deep channels filled with gurgling brooks. Lambley is tucked away at the bottom of a small valley surrounded by a rolling patchwork quilt of fields and clumps of woodland. Lambley derives from 'Lambs' Lea' – an enclosure for the grazing of sheep – although much of the surrounding land is now given over to arable production.

Altogether the rural scene laid out before you is one of such total peace and tranquillity that it might come as a bit of a shock to discover that the bustling city of Nottingham is only 8 miles (12.9km) away.

## Cowslip Sunday

Lambley was once well known in this part of Nottinghamshire because of its wild flowers, and to this day its symbol remains the cowslip. The first Sunday of May was traditionally known as Cowslip Sunday, when crowds would come to the dumbles around Lambley to gather cowslips for wine making. (Incidentally, did you know that many wild and garden flowers – including dandelion, elderflower, marigold, wallflower and rose petals – are still used in country wine making?) Over the years, the Cowslip Sunday gathering grew to become a huge annual event, often attracting thousands of people from the working-class areas of Nottingham. Stalls of food and drink were set up in the main street, and the festivities lasted all day.

Sadly, and rather inevitably, the cowslips themselves didn't last too long, for although the roots may not be disturbed the actual picking of the flowers prevents seeds ripening and scattering, and so the colony does not renew itself. Although they are now protected by law – it is illegal to pick them – the tubular yellow flowers of the cowslip are becoming scarcer still, since the demise of Cowslip Sunday in the mid-1900s was also a result of the increased ploughing of the old pasture where they used to thrive.

# LAMBLEY

Hope springs eternal, as they say, and to the north of Lambley Dumble, just beyond the playing field, is an example of how the countryside can be changed for the better. With the help of the Woodland Trust, Bonney Doles was planted in a day by local people in December 1998. Apart from the new woods, a large area of traditional meadow has been retained, and it is hoped that, by careful annual mowing, cowslips and other wild flowers will be encouraged to recolonise the area.

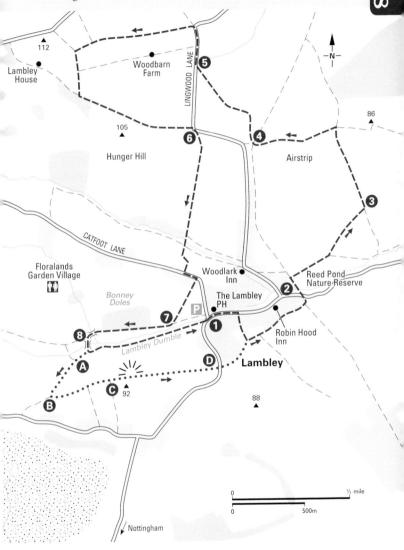

## WALK 18 DIRECTIONS

❶ From The Lambley pub, walk down Main Street into the centre of the village. In 220yds (210m) go right for a public footpath between houses and around the edge of a fenced field. Turn left at the end and go over successive stiles (at the second take the left-hand choice of two) for a path behind houses. Turn left at the end to drop down, cross

## WHAT TO LOOK FOR

Bonney Doles is one of more than 200 new Community Woods created by the Woodland Trust as part of the Millennium Commission-funded 'Woods on your Doorstep' project. The Woodland Trust is Britain's leading woodland conservation charity, and since 1972 has planted more than five million trees and established nearly 700 new woods.

the road, and enter Reed Pond Nature Reserve.

**2** Veer left to reach the gate in the far left corner. Turn right and out along the bottom of several large fields, cutting across the lower part of the second. Continue around the edge of a copse and when you reach a large sloping field ahead of you, turn left.

**3** Follow the wide track uphill to the left of the hedge. In the far corner of the third field, with a grassy airstrip along its middle, turn left (not the footpath straight on) and walk along the field-edge.

**4** Just before it ends go right and, following the direction of the footpath post (not the bridleway), aim half left across the next field then bear left across pasture. Drop down the hillside, aiming for the stile beyond the wooden enclosure in the far corner by the road.

**5** Turn right and walk along the roadside verge past Woodbarn

## WHILE YOU'RE THERE

A mile (1.6km) up Catfoot Lane is Floralands Garden Village, a vast site that includes specialist camping, aquatic and garden suppliers. There's a well-stocked gift shop at the back of the main garden centre, plus public toilets and the Jasmine Tea Rooms.

Farm to the sharp right-hand bend. Go left across the top of successive fields to reach the wooded track on the far side. Turn left here and stay on this path as it bends left and becomes a wide trail which leads all the way back to the junction with Lingwood Lane.

**6** Turn right, cross a field (aiming half left), then follow the waymarks down through three fields into the woodland at the bottom. Go straight on via a footbridge, left into a field on the far side, then almost immediately right and walk up through a field to the top. Climb the steps and turn left on to the road for 100yds (91m), then go right beside a bungalow to drop down diagonally right across ridged fields to the football pitch.

## WHERE TO EAT AND DRINK

There are three pubs in Lambley. The Woodlark Inn (closed Monday) on Church Street and Robin Hood Inn on Main Street both serve traditional pub food, while The Lambley, at the start of the walk, offers more sophisticated cuisine. There is also the Jasmine Tea Rooms at Floralands Garden Village.

**7** At the far corner continue on a popular (and obvious) path to walk through a newly planted woodland area known as Bonney Doles. Go over a footbridge, turn left, and follow the field-edge to the corner.

**8** Here a short path with a handrail ventures into the bumpy wooded dell for a short way. Ignore this and continue around to cross another footbridge. Turn left and follow the path through the woods, then the field bottom along the south side of Lambley Dumble, eventually turning left on to Spring Lane to return to the car park.

# A Lambley Loop

*Add this extra section for hilltop views back over the Dumbles.*
**See map and information panel for Walk 18**

WALK 19

DISTANCE 7.75 miles (12.5km)   MINIMUM TIME 3hrs 30min
ASCENT/GRADIENT 623ft (190m) ▲▲▲   LEVEL OF DIFFICULTY +++

## WALK 19 DIRECTIONS
## (Walk 18 option)

Go over the second Lambley Dumble footbridge beyond Point ❽, but instead of turning left for the path back to the village, turn right and follow the path alongside then diagonally left across a rough meadow. Go over a stile (Point Ⓐ) and continue the route uphill through a long, sloping field, aiming just to the left of the brow of the hill ahead.

Cross a second, much shorter field to reach a stile and a pleasant hedged track (Point Ⓑ). Turn left and follow this long and quite narrow thoroughfare for 0.25 mile (400m).

Go across the driveway to a house and continue on the far side, past some more buildings (Point Ⓒ), then go out across the right-hand edge of wide, high fields. There are excellent views down to Lambley Dumble, with its twisting course along the valley bottom marked by a thin but dense strip of trees. Beyond is the new plantation of Bonney Doles, with the area of shrubs and saplings to the top of the enclosure.

The final field dips down to the road and, as the hedge falls away to the right, walk straight ahead across the middle of the field (aiming for the final house on the road into Lambley). Drop down to the stile that sits in the gap in the hedge at the bottom (Point Ⓓ).

Go across the road for the rough lane opposite, signposted 'public footpath', along the end of a row of back gardens. After 275yds (251m) take the path off to the left, past the fenced field and between houses, that you originally set off from.

Go left on to Main Street to return to the start.

---

### WHAT TO LOOK FOR
Although the only local industry in Lambley today appears to be agriculture, there was once a flourishing textile business, and many of the former workers' cottages can be seen alongside the brooks and culverts. Records show that although Flemish weavers were present here as far back as the 15th century, it wasn't until the mid-1800s that a boom in framework knitting brought prosperity to Lambley – and at one time there were as many as 381 machines at work in the village. Increasing mechanisation and the rise of the large urban mills and factories eventually sealed the fate of the village businesses.

# A Trundle Above the Trent

*Enjoy a pleasant rural stretch
of Nottinghamshire's premier river.*

WALK 20

---

| | |
|---|---|
| **DISTANCE** 5.5 miles (8.8km) | **MINIMUM TIME** 3hrs |
| **ASCENT/GRADIENT** 722ft (220m) ▲▲▲ | **LEVEL OF DIFFICULTY** ✦✦✦ |

**PATHS** Field tracks and riverside meadow, may be flooded after heavy rain, 8 stiles, steep steps

**LANDSCAPE** Wide river plain backed by steep banks

**SUGGESTED MAP** OS Explorer 260 Nottingham

**START/FINISH** Grid reference: SK 691431

**DOG FRIENDLINESS** On lead near livestock, fine elsewhere (note stiles)

**PARKING** Kerbside in centre of East Bridgford (Main Street or Kneeton Road)

**PUBLIC TOILETS** None on route (except for pub customers)

---

## WALK 20 DIRECTIONS

From the centre of East Bridgford, by the crossroads below the church, walk along Kneeton Road out of the village past the Reindeer Inn. Just past Lammas Farm, with the stump of an old brick windmill (built in 1841) ahead, turn left on to a wide, semi-surfaced lane indicated 'public bridleway'. Ignore a footpath turning on the right and continue down this track, bending right in 0.25 mile (400m) at a junction of paths where an open gate and track invites you to go straight on. Now follow this airy, undulating route, which offers fantastic views over the Trent Valley, for about 0.75 mile (1.2km). In the sky you might see light aircraft and gliders from the nearby airfield at Syerston.

Beyond Old Hill, with its communications mast, the track becomes a narrowing path and drops steeply downhill. Before it bends sharply left, towards the bottom, go across a stile on your right for a clearly indicated path steeply uphill by a line of hawthorn trees. At the far side of the field continue along the level edge of another, then at a junction of routes by a high cross-hedge turn left on to a footpath signposted 'Kneeton'. Go along the edge of successive fields, switching to the adjacent (left) field approaching the village and, via the metal gate at the end, for a lane to reach the simple but beautiful Church of St Helen.

Turn left beyond the church (you'll notice that the churchyard is in fact almost circular) for a shady, sunken lane that drops down to the floodplain. Go over the stile at the bottom and out across Trent

---

### WHERE TO EAT AND DRINK

The Reindeer Inn, on the Kneeton Road out of East Bridgford, serves food daily from Tuesday to Saturday, specialising in simple home-cooked dishes like Scotch eggs, fish cakes and Lincolnshire sausages. Just over the Trent bridge (off the A6097), the Unicorn Hotel and the Anchor Inn are family pubs serving meals daily.

# EAST BRIDGFORD

Meadows with the wide river to your right. There is a vaguely discernible track across the grass, but just aim for the stile and gate in the middle of the cross-fence almost 0.5 mile (800m) ahead, then continue ahead through the second wide field. Where the pasture ends, at the very far side, go over a stile ahead (not the one uphill to the left) and turn right for a path around the bottom of a small, fenced-off plantation. The river flows languidly past to your right.

In only 100yds (91m) you climb a low bank and go over the stile on the left (indicated 'Parish Paths Partnership') which leads into the enclosure and up a steep track among the young trees and shrubs. Climb the steps and stay on this path as it swings right and finally emerges in the corner of an open field. Turn right and walk along the bottom of a succession of large fields for over a mile (1.6km), keeping parallel with the river now some way below on your right.

You have to follow the field-edge away from the river to skirt several large wooded gullies (like walking a coast path and having to veer inland around coves and inlets). The first and third require you to descend and then climb some steps among the trees, and the second needs quite a diversion away from the Trent and back. All the time stick to the side of the field and follow the waymarking arrows.

About 0.25 mile (400m) beyond the second series of steps a public footpath is indicated to the right. This drops sharply down steps through the trees to the river bank, where you can turn left to follow a public footpath beside the water along to the weir. It offers a different perspective on the river, but the vegetation can be quite high in the summer and the route is liable to winter flooding.

Alternatively continue along the field-edge to the far end, then go through a gate, around a paddock, and down the driveway of a small mobile-home park. To inspect the river at first hand – you will have heard and glimpsed its mighty weir thundering away for some time – turn right at the bottom for the short track past the marina. This is where the bankside path comes out.

Cross over the road near the marina and mobile-home entrance, then go left, through a kissing gate (not the public footpath straight on). A notice board explains about the motte-and-bailey castle located near by. Follow this obvious and easy route up alongside the road until it drops down to join it just before the church in the middle of East Bridgford.

# King of Belvoir Castle

*Discover a fairy-tale castle and a lost canal on the Lincs–Leics border.*

DISTANCE *4.75 miles (7.7km)*  MINIMUM TIME *2hrs*

ASCENT/GRADIENT *230ft (70m)* ▲▲▲  LEVEL OF DIFFICULTY +++

PATHS *Tow path, field and woodland tracks and country lane, 2 stiles*

LANDSCAPE *Steep wooded hills and open arable land*

SUGGESTED MAP *OS Explorer 247 Grantham*

START/FINISH *Grid reference: SK 837342*

DOG FRIENDLINESS *Excellent, under close control near livestock*

PARKING *Main Street in Woolsthorpe by Belvoir*

PUBLIC TOILETS *None on route (nearest in Grantham)*

First, the small matter of pronunciation. In these parts 'Belvoir' sounds like 'Beaver', although quite why this should be is unclear because its history dates back to Norman times when William the Conqueror gave the land to his standard-bearer Robert de Todeni. The original castle was called 'Belvedere', a term still used in landscape architecture to denote an elevated room offering good views. Belvoir Castle passed through many hands over the centuries, and was virtually destroyed on more than one occasion. The most recent was during the Civil War, when Woolsthorpe's original church was also reduced to rubble (the present one dates from 1848).

In 1508 the castle came into the hands of the Manners family, and is currently home to the latest in the line, the 11th Duke of Rutland. However the present castle dates mainly from the early 19th century and is in the 'romantic' style of the day, with elaborate turrets and battlements.

Both the castle and its grounds are open to the public from Easter to September (visit www.belvoircastle.com for precise opening times). There is an impressive collection of artwork and period furniture, costumed guides giving a glimpse of life 'below stairs', and a restaurant and ice-cream parlour. Regular special events are held throughout the summer including country fairs, concerts and medieval jousting.

## A Lost Canal

In contrast to the bustle and activity of the Grand Union Canal at Foxton Locks (see Walk 27), the Grantham Canal appears rather forlorn and overlooked. It was built 1793–7 and provided a 33-mile (53km) link between Nottingham and Grantham via Leicestershire. Despite competition from the Nottingham–Grantham railway it was initially profitable, and was used to transport local produce such as iron ore from the hills above Woolsthorpe, which was taken via the Trent and the Erewash Canal to the ironworks at Ilkeston. But the waterway's business was finally dashed by the construction of the (now defunct) Belvoir branch ironstone railway in 1883, which you can see running parallel with the canal to join the Nottingham–Grantham line to the north.

# BELVOIR

The canal was abandoned in 1936 and, despite the intentions of a restoration trust to make it navigable, it is now a quiet and largely overlooked thoroughfare. There are clear stretches, and British Waterways has kept most of the permissive tow path in a walkable state, but in places the weeds and rushes and luxuriant vegetation have almost choked the waterway.

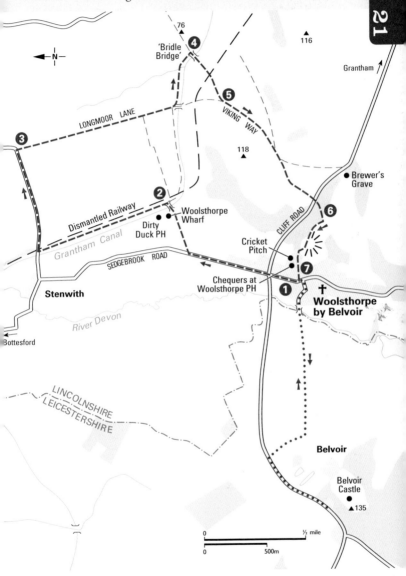

## WALK 21 DIRECTIONS

❶ Walk northwards out of the village of Woolsthorpe by Belvoir on the pavement of Sedgebrook Road, the continuation of Main Street, towards Bottesford. Turn right into the wide-verged lane for the Rutland Arms public house (signposted) and cross over the canal bridge at Woolsthorpe Wharf.

**2** Turn left and follow the straight, grassy bank along the Grantham Canal until Stenwith Bridge (No 60). Climb the steps to your right, just before reaching the bridge, and turn right on to the road. Follow this over the old railway bridge and out along a lovely wide lane of oak trees. After 700yds (640m) it bends left, and here turn right.

### WHILE YOU'RE THERE

The attractive 12th-century St Mary the Virgin Church at Bottesford has the highest spire in Leicestershire (210ft/64m). The tombs and effigies of the various incumbents of Belvoir Castle include that of Francis, the 6th Earl of Rutland, who lies between his first and second wives. Two of his sons are recorded as dying by witchcraft.

**3** Follow the initially hedged and unmade Longmoor Lane for just over 0.75 mile (1.2km). When you reach the far end turn left before the bridge, to join the gravel tow path, and walk along this as far as an elegant wooden arched bridge ('Bridle Bridge').

**4** Cross over the bridge and head out across the middle of a wide arable field. Go over the course of

### WHERE TO EAT AND DRINK

The two popular local pubs both serve food lunchtime and evening and offer outdoor seating. The Chequers at Woolsthorpe, off Woolsthorpe's Main Street, is a handsome old country pub overlooking the cricket pitch, while the Dirty Duck (formerly Rutland Arms Inn) is located a mile (1.6km) north of the village by the canal and includes a large outdoor play area for children. Belvoir Castle has a restaurant and ice-cream parlour for visitors.

the old railway again and continue up the left-hand side of a sloping field. At the top, turn left on to a well-walked track.

**5** Follow this pleasant route with lovely views out towards the hills surrounding Grantham. Where the track kinks left, after a fenced section, go straight on right across a wide field – follow the direction of the public footpath signpost and aim for the hedge opening at the very far side. Go across Cliff Road for a track into woodland.

**6** At the far side of the woods, cross the stile and turn right to follow the field-edge down the bumpy, grassy slope back to Woolsthorpe. There are excellent views across the head of the Vale of Belvoir to Belvoir Castle opposite. At the bottom of the slope go over the stile behind the cricket scorebox, along the edge of the pitch (the football ground to your left), and down the drive of the pub to reach the village centre.

### WHAT TO LOOK FOR

Towards the end of the walk, on the wooded hilltop east of Woolsthorpe, is a place marked as Brewer's Grave, so called because it is believed to be the last resting place of an unfortunate brewer from Belvoir Castle who one night drank too much and accidentally drowned in a vat of his own ale.

**7** If you want to extend the walk to visit Belvoir Castle, turn left into Main Street, then right into Belvoir Lane. At the end of this cul-de-sac go over a small bridge and continue ahead across fields towards the hilltop fortification. After the third stile, cross another stile to your right and follow this wide track uphill to the road, then turn left to the castle entrance.

# Mad for the West Leake Hills

*Explore a dubious case of insanity among the panoramic West Leake Hills, south of Nottingham.*

**DISTANCE** 4.25 miles (6.8km)  **MINIMUM TIME** 2hrs

**ASCENT/GRADIENT** 246ft (75m) ▲▲▲  **LEVEL OF DIFFICULTY** +++

**PATHS** Field-edge paths, farm lanes and forest tracks, 3 stiles

**LANDSCAPE** Wooded ridge of hills surrounded by open arable land

**SUGGESTED MAP** OS Explorer 246 Loughborough

**START/FINISH** Grid reference: SK 527264

**DOG FRIENDLINESS** Generally good on woodland tracks and wide farm lanes

**PARKING** Roadside parking near West Leake church

**PUBLIC TOILETS** None on route (nearest in East Leake)

The villages of East and West Leake, located near Nottinghamshire's border with Leicestershire, were recorded in the Domesday Book as 'Leche'. The name comes from the Anglo-Saxon word meaning 'water-meadow', since both lie on Kingston Brook, a tributary of the River Soar. Although the Church of St Helena in West Leake has medieval origins, it has been extensively modernised, and includes a tiny bellcote (with two bells) rather than the usual spire or squat tower. In the churchyard you will find a 'living willow seat', which, as its name suggests, is a wooden bench with a back made of live willow.

## Completely Cuckoo?

North of the West Leake Hills is the village of Gotham (pronounced 'Goatem'), and in medieval times a group of purported lunatics lived in the woods near by. Today, near Leake New Wood, the names of Cuckoo Bush Farm and Cuckoo Bush Wood record their strange antics, for according to folklore the so-called Gotham Fools tried to hedge-in a cuckoo so it would sing to them all year (it flew off, of course). They also burned down a forge to rid it of a wasps' nest, and tried to drown fish in buckets.

Their bizarre activities were later detailed in a book entitled *The Merrie Tales of the Mad Men of Gottam* (1630) and developed into something of a folk story, so that 'cuckoo pens' became a joke name given to small hillside crofts or enclosures. The book describes the events at Gotham:

> 'On a time the men of Gottam would have pinned in the Cuckoo, whereby shee should sing all the yeere, and in the midst of the town they made a hedge round in compasse, and they had got a Cuckoo, and had her put into it, and said, Sing here all the yeere, and thou shalt lacke neither meat nor drinke. The Cuckoo as soon as she perceived her self incompassed within the hedge, flew away. A vengeance on her said they, We made not our hedge high enough.'

# WEST LEAKE HILLS

However, their apparent madness was not quite what it seemed, for according to local sources it was a deliberate ruse to deter the visiting emissaries of King John, who wanted to build a royal hunting lodge on their village land. They reasoned that the King would want nothing to do with a community of lunatics, but whether this was true or just an attempt at face-saving has been lost to time. Gotham is still remembered for its madmen, and the village pub is even called the Cuckoo Bush. As an old nursery rhyme goes:

> 'Three wise men of Gotham
> Went to sea in a bowl.
> If the bowl had been stronger
> My story would have been longer.'

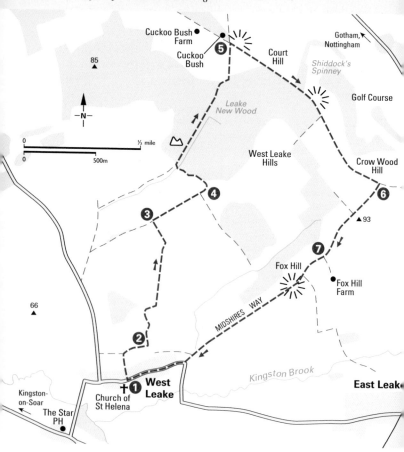

## WALK 22 DIRECTIONS

**1** Walk across the road from the church, half-way along West Leake's main street, to cross the stile opposite. Go between houses and directly out across an open

field. Go over the stile at the far side and turn right to follow the field-edge path to the end.

**2** Go through to the next field and turn left. Now follow a clear route alongside the hedge, past a

68

# WEST LEAKE HILLS

West Leake's pub is The Star, on Melton Lane, just to the south-west of the village. It's known locally as Leake Pit House, since it once incorporated a pit for cock-fighting. The pub is more than 200 years old, with an open fire in winter and colourful hanging baskets in the summer.

vegetation-choked pond (often dry in summer), and out across the middle of subsequent fields on an obvious farm track. Far away to the left are the massive cooling towers of Ratcliffe-on-Soar power station – quite a juxtaposition to the lovely countryside immediately about, don't you think.

**3** When you arrive at a wide gravel track, turn right and follow this as far as the edge of the woods, marked by a yellow-topped public bridleway sign and a notice warning you to go no further.

**4** Go left before the hedge and after 275yds (251m) turn right for a bridleway route (waymarked with blue arrows) up the steep hillside between the trees. At the top this becomes a clear, straight path through the attractive mixed woodland of Leake New Wood. When you reach the far side go

## WHAT TO LOOK FOR

As you stand on Court Hill, gazing out over a largely rural South Nottinghamshire, you may be surprised to discover that far below your feet is an important gypsum mine (the large works, near East Leake, are partially glimpsed a little further on). Gypsum, or hydrated calcium sulphate, is used for making cement and plaster, including plaster of Paris. Its many forms include selenite (transparent), satin spar (fibrous) and alabaster (used for ornaments).

through a gate and cross to the far side of the field.

**5** At a junction of bridle paths, go through the gate and turn right to walk along the initially open hilltop, with expansive views to your left over the Trent Valley towards Gotham and distant Nottingham. Continue along this easy, panoramic route via Court Hill for almost 1 mile (1.6km). Beyond the trees of Shiddock's Spinney a golf course appears on your left. At a fork of paths keep right so that you end up alongside the arable field on your right and not the fairway on your left.

## WHILE YOU'RE THERE

A couple of miles (3.2km) from West Leake is the village of Kingston-on-Soar, where the Church of St Winifred's contains an elaborate monument dedicated to the local Babington family, involving columns covered with intricate tracery. In 1586 Antony Babington led a failed plot to put Mary, Queen of Scots on the throne. He paid for the deed with his head.

**6** At Crow Wood Hill you reach the bend of a semi-surfaced lane. Turn right and follow its south-westerly route across the open fields of Fox Hill, with wide views over to the red-tile roofs of East Leake.

**7** When the drive turns into Fox Hill Farm go straight on along a clear field-edge track ahead, and ignoring a path off to the left, follow this long, straight route back down to West Leake. The vista now stretches out southwards, where the wooded ridges of Charnwood Forest (especially Beacon Hill and Bradgate Park) dominate the skyline. At the road junction at the bottom go straight on for the centre of the village.

# Among the Deer at Bradgate

*Leicester's scenic Bradgate Park offers
a range of enjoyable walks for all ages.*

WALK 23

| | |
|---|---|
| **DISTANCE** 3.75 miles (6km) | **MINIMUM TIME** 1hr 45min |
| **ASCENT/GRADIENT** 558ft (170m) ▲▲▲ | **LEVEL OF DIFFICULTY** ✦✦✦ |

**PATHS** *Easy surfaced tracks and undulating paths, 2 stiles*
**LANDSCAPE** *Rolling parkland of woods and open spaces*
**SUGGESTED MAP** *OS Explorer 246 Loughborough*
**START/FINISH** *Grid reference: SK 522098*
**DOG FRIENDLINESS** *On lead near deer, good in Swithland Wood (Walk 24)*
**PARKING** *Car park at Newtown Linford (pay-and-display)*
**PUBLIC TOILETS** *By car parks at start and Hallgates, and visitor centre*

Bradgate Park lies just to the north-west of Leicester, and is a popular place of escape for the city's population. The spacious and diverse nature of the park's 840 acres (340ha) make it a great family venue, offering easy surfaced tracks and open grassy tracts through to more adventurous hillside paths across the heath, bracken and rocky outcrops.

## The Nine-day Queen

The centrepiece of the original park was Bradgate House, now just a few sorry ruins. It was built at the turn of the 16th century and was home to the Grey family. Henry Grey was created Duke of Suffolk in 1551, and because (through his wife) his three daughters were the grandchildren of Mary, Henry VIII's younger sister, they had a distant claim to the throne. But the distance grew considerably shorter when a dying Edward VI was persuaded to alter the succession to disinherit Catholic Mary, and instead the eldest of the three daughters, Lady Jane Grey, was proclaimed queen in July 1553 even though she was an unwilling player in events. Just nine days later the scheming Duke of Northumberland had her deposed and imprisoned in the Tower of London. Barely seven months on, the innocent 16-year-old girl was beheaded. According to legend, when the news of her execution reached Bradgate, her childhood home, the groundsmen lopped the tops of the oak trees, and to this day stumpy, pollarded oak trees scatter the park.

## Doe, a Deer, a Female Deer...

Although Bradgate Park was given over to public recreation in the 1930s, it continues to support a resident fallow and red deer population of around 300. Deer have been kept here since the 13th century and you'll probably be able to get some close-up views of the handsome creatures. Signs warn against feeding the animals, and it goes without saying that dogs must be kept under tight control when there are deer about.

Bear in mind that deer, like sheep, can carry ticks, and in the summer months when the bracken and grass are high these irritating little mites can also transfer themselves to human skin. If you discover one on your person remove it carefully, but better still avoid getting bitten in the first place by wearing long trousers and a long-sleeved top, and making sure you check yourself and your children at the end of your walk. The park authority produces a helpful leaflet on the subject, available from the visitor centre.

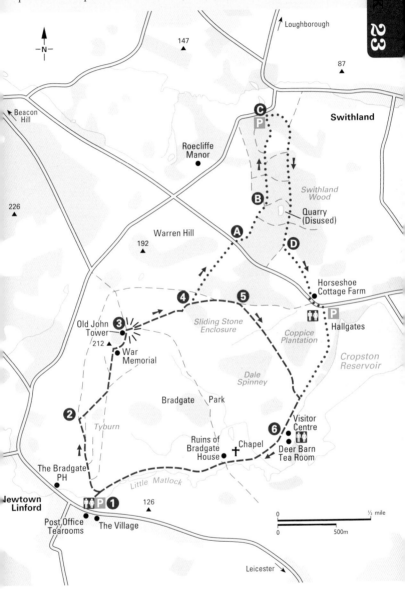

## WALK 23 DIRECTIONS

❶ Enter the grounds from the large car park at Newtown Linford and turn sharply left on a wide track. Go through an open gateway

and, ignoring paths off to the right, stick on the main route uphill (there are in fact two parallel tracks), keeping the park's boundary wall in sight on your left.

*Overleaf: Bradgate Park (Walk 23)*

**WALK 23**

**2** When you draw level with a large wooden swing gate in the wall, fork right. Go steadily uphill on a wide grassy ride through the banks of bracken, past a small plantation known as Tyburn, and soon you will see the prominent hilltop war memorial up ahead on your left. Follow the obvious grassy track all the way to reach the 'summit', then go round to the right of the walled plantation behind it to reach the folly known as Old John Tower. Although the centre of Leicester is only 6 miles (9.7km) away, the extensive views from this excellent viewpoint (695ft/212m) are predominantly rural, with large tracts of woodland scattered about.

### WHILE YOU'RE THERE

For more stimulating walking and another lofty country park viewpoint, visit Beacon Hill, about 3 miles (4.8km) to the north of Bradgate, near Woodhouse Eaves. There was once a Bronze-Age settlement around the 815-ft (248m) summit, and now you too can gaze over the Trent and Soar valleys in search of warring tribes, sabre-tooth tigers and ice-cream vans.

**3** Turn right, straight down the hillside, to a small circular pond in the bracken below. Take the left of three paths on the far side and continue to reach a track around a walled plantation known as Sliding Stone Enclosure. Turn left and walk along this track for 100yds (91m).

**4** Ignore the path straight down to the gate in the wall on your left (see Walk 24), and instead go straight on. The grassy track drops down to reach the park's boundary wall, then continues uphill on a short tarmac strip past a small underground reservoir.

### WHERE TO EAT AND DRINK

The Bradgate Park Tea Room, beside the car park, is open Tuesday to Sunday in summer and Thursday to Sunday in winter. The Deer Barn Tea Room at the visitor centre is open similar hours. The Post Office Tea Rooms and The Village bistro are both opposite the park entrance, and The Bradgate pub serves food lunchtimes and evenings.

**5** After 125yds (114m) take the track off to the right, by a wooden bench and, rather incongruously, two drainage covers. This long, straight grassy track heads across the middle of the country park and is easy to follow. It passes between Coppice Plantation and Dale Spinney, from where there are good views across Cropston Reservoir. Continue all the way down to reach the surfaced drive at the bottom and turn right to the visitor centre (open April to October).

**6** Continue along this easy, tarmac route past the ruins of Bradgate House and the restored chapel, then on alongside the pools and waterfalls of a small valley known as Little Matlock. Look out for the monkey puzzle tree and the cedar of Lebanon, introduced to the park in the 19th century. Continue all the way back to the car park.

### WHAT TO LOOK FOR

In the centre of the park, next to the main path, is the ruined outline of Bradgate House. Built from the late 1400s, it was one of the first fortified mansions made entirely from brick, with two main wings and towers at the corners (the stumps of a couple are still standing), linked by a great hall that opened out into a courtyard.

# A Swithland Wood Loop

*Add this circuit of SwithlandWood for a longer day at Bradgate Park.*
**See map and information panel for Walk 23**

WALK 24

**DISTANCE** 6 miles (9.7km)  **MINIMUM TIME** 3hrs
**ASCENT/GRADIENT** 656ft (200m) ▲▲▲  **LEVEL OF DIFFICULTY** ✦✦✦

## WALK 24 DIRECTIONS
(Walk 23 option)

Leave Walk 23 at Point ❹ and from the enclosure drop straight down to leave the park via the gate and stile opposite for a long, straight farm track down to the road (Point **Ⓐ**). Cross this, and go through the gap in the wall for the short path straight ahead (not right), then turn left on to the main track through the woods, keeping the perimeter wall to the left in sight. Eventually you drop down to a small clearing with a wooden litter bin and three tracks going off ahead (Point **Ⓑ**). Take the one on the left (it's behind the sign pointing right for horses), then within a few paces fork left again by a wooden post.

Swithland Wood is a remnant of Charnwood Forest, once a medieval hunting chase and today full of mature oak, birch, lime and alder.

Follow the direct route for 0.25 mile (400m) and, just after rounding a small hill, aim for the open field glimpsed ahead. Take the path along its left-hand edge and, at the end, turn left on a wider track to reach Swithland Wood North car park (Point **Ⓒ**).

Go beyond the bar gate and turn right on a narrow path parallel with the road, which climbs beside a fence overlooking a flooded quarry. On the far side fork right to join a wider track along the woodland edge. This main route bears right and heads directly south through the lovely mixed woods for almost 0.75 mile (1.2km), and is helpfully indicated by yellow markers on posts that denote a horse-riding route. Ignore all other routes off left and right.

On the way you pass another fenced-off, flooded quarry where the much sought-after Swithland slate was quarried as far back as Roman times. It was only supplanted by the thinner and cheaper Welsh slate quite recently.

Eventually a field appears on the left (Point **Ⓓ**). Go down the steps on the left on to a boundary path, then in 100yds (91m) cross the bridge and stile on the right over a stream. Turn half left across the wide field, aiming for the gate and stile in the far corner by Horseshoe Cottage Farm. Here turn left to walk the roadside verge to Hallgates car park, then re-enter Bradgate Park for the surfaced track ahead to the visitor centre (Point ❻) and back to Newtown Linford.

# The New National Forest

*An introduction to a new forest taking shape in Leicestershire.*

| | |
|---|---|
| **DISTANCE** 4 miles (6.4km) | **MINIMUM TIME** 1hr 45min |
| **ASCENT/GRADIENT** 130ft (40m) ▲▲▲ | **LEVEL OF DIFFICULTY** +++ |
| **PATHS** Woodland and field tracks, 5 stiles | |
| **LANDSCAPE** Mixed woodland and landscaped parks | |
| **SUGGESTED MAP** OS Explorer 245 The National Forest | |
| **START/FINISH** Grid reference: SK 329141 | |
| **DOG FRIENDLINESS** Good throughout, but careful on roads | |
| **PARKING** Oakthorpe picnic area, Ashby Road, off B586 at Donisthorpe (note closing times) | |
| **PUBLIC TOILETS** None on route (nearest in Ashby de la Zouch) | |

## WALK 25 DIRECTIONS

From the car park walk along the surfaced track as far as the site of the former colliery. Only the capped pitheads give any indication that this pleasant rural spot was once an industrial hub. Go left and follow the unmade path through the trees and veer left to the lake. On the far side leave the gravel track and walk along the open, grassy northern shore. Ignore the public footpath off to the left and continue beyond the water and along the left-hand side of a newly planted area.

Willesley Wood is centred on what was once Oakthorpe Colliery and is now owned by the Woodland Trust. Since 1991, when it became one of the first National Forest planting sites, more than 75,000 trees and shrubs have been planted here. Altogether the Woodland Trust owns 17 separate woods in the National Forest, most of which have been newly created in areas previously devoid of extensive tree cover.

About 100yds (91m) before you reach the gate to the lane, turn right. Walk past the notice board (explaining that the local Royal British Legion has created this new grove as an area of remembrance) and along a gravel path into the woods. On the far side go straight out along a wide grassy ride (not right, beside the woods), then in 50yds (46m) branch first right. Ignoring a fork to the left, continue to the end and turn left on to another grassy track. At the top of this go right, along a narrow path between gorse and bracken that opens out into the long and straight Pastures Lane.

The National Forest covers around 200 square miles (518sq km) of Leicestershire, Staffordshire and Derbyshire, and since its inception in the early 1990s more than 7 million of the projected 30 million new trees have been planted. Of course this is a long-term project, so don't expect a continuous swathe of woodland across the East Midlands for some years to come!

# THE NATIONAL FOREST

The ambitious plan aims to blend pockets of ancient woodland, such as Charnwood and Needwood, with new broadleaved (60 per cent) and coniferous (40 per cent) plantations. Many of the new sites in north-west Leicestershire, like here at Willesley and Saltersford, are former coal mines that were abandoned after flooding, but the ensuing subsidence has since created artificial lakes or 'flashes', and large-scale reclamation projects have helped nature recolonise these former industrial zones.

## WHAT TO LOOK FOR

The National Forest 'Plant a Tree' scheme invites people to adopt a newly planted tree. In return you are invited to the planting event, receive an 'adopters pack' and an annual update on the growth and development of your woodland, plus details on sightings of animals, insects and plants seen there. For more information pick up a leaflet at Conkers Discovery Centre.

At the very far end of Pastures Lane, cross Measham Road and walk along New Street. Turn right at the end, opposite The Holly Bush pub, then branch off ahead / right down Canal Street. At the turning bay at the end turn right on a public footpath along the bottom of a rough field. Half way across go through the gate on the left for a path through the trees into Saltersford Valley Picnic Area. (If this path is too overgrown, continue to the gate and path at the far corner of the field and turn left here.) Go left on to the main path for the easy loop of the woodland and lakes.

When you have completed the short circuit and reached the main picnic area by the notice board go right and, at the circular car park, continue out on to Measham Road. Cross over to the pavement and turn right then, just past the 30mph sign, turn left for a public footpath across two fields. After crossing the second diagonally to the left – aiming for the yellow-topped post on the far side – veer half right to join a bumpy and overgrown path past Lowlands Farm. The path keeps to the left of a small lake, with hawthorn trees in-between, and although narrow continues through patchy vegetation. After the second stile turn left to return to the capped pitheads and the path back to the car park.

Just to the west of Oakthorpe the trackbed of the Ashby and Nuneaton Joint Railway has been transformed into the Ashby Woulds Heritage Trail. This runs north via the former Donisthorpe Colliery (now converted into a woodland park) and the preserved Moira Furnace, built in 1806 for iron-making and now a fascinating visitor attraction. It ends close to the Conkers Discovery Centre, near Moira (follow the signs on the trail or road), which is where you can learn much more about the National Forest. The huge site includes interactive exhibits, craft workshops, outdoor woodland trails and assault courses. If your children still have surplus energy left after the walk, let them go bonkers at Conkers!

## WHERE TO EAT AND DRINK

If you want a good local pub, try The Masons Arms on the crossroads at Donisthorpe and The Holly Bush at Oakthorpe. The tea rooms at Moira Furnace and the café and restaurant at Conkers Discovery Centre are both family-friendly. For a wider choice visit Ashby de la Zouch, 2.5 miles (4km) away.

# Doing Battle at Bosworth

*Visit Bosworth — one of England's most famous battlefield sites — via a country park and a canal tow path.*

**DISTANCE** 8.25 miles (14.1km)   **MINIMUM TIME** 4hrs

**ASCENT/GRADIENT** 279ft (85m) ▲▲▲   **LEVEL OF DIFFICULTY** +++

**PATHS** Easy lanes and tow path, may be muddy, 8 stiles

**LANDSCAPE** Gently rolling woods and arable land

**SUGGESTED MAP** OS Explorers 232 Nuneaton & Tamworth; 233 Leicester & Hinckley

**START/FINISH** Grid reference: SK 412031 (on Explorer 232)

**DOG FRIENDLINESS** Generally very good (care on street sections)

**PARKING** Market Bosworth Country Park (pay-and-display)

**PUBLIC TOILETS** At car park, Bosworth Battlefield Heritage Centre, Shenton Station and Market Bosworth

The Battle of Bosworth Field, which took place on 22 August 1485, is one of the key events in English history. Not did it only finally bring to an end the long-running Wars of the Roses, but it also signalled the beginning of a new era, as the Middle Ages gave way to the powerful Tudor dynasty.

The Yorkist Richard III had only been ruler for a couple of years before Henry Tudor landed in Pembrokeshire with a small and rather ragbag force and advanced on the Midlands. The two armies met at Ambion Hill, south of Market Bosworth, with Richard's larger force occupying the higher ground and Henry's scattered below. Nowadays their positions are marked by their standards which flutter from tall flagpoles. A third standard, located some way to the north, belonged to a faction led by Sir William Stanley, who crucially decided to pitch in on Henry's side at the last moment and, in so doing, tipped the scales by cutting off and surrounding the King. Richard was defeated and Henry Tudor became Henry VII of England.

There are interpretative panels all the way along the 1.75-mile (2.8km) Battle Trail, showing the position of the armies and how the fateful day unfurled. The fascinating exhibition at the heritage centre (closed January) is supplemented by regular workshops and re-enactments by local groups throughout the summer months.

## The Controversial Monarch

A memorial stone now marks the place where Richard was slain, but as the last of the Plantagenets — and indeed the last king of England to die in battle — he's since received something of a bad press from historians and chroniclers, most notably William Shakespeare. In fact largely thanks to Shakespeare's play there are few more villainous characters in English literature than Richard III ('I can smile, and murder while I smile'), but whether the reputation is deserved is doubtful. Although he may have been involved previously in the infamous murder of the Little Princes in the Tower, there is scant evidence to suggest that he was any worse as a king than other rulers of the time, plus he seemed to be an able administrator and leader. There is even a society established to clear Richard's name and they meet every year, around the date of the battle, at the Church of St James in nearby Sutton Cheney, where the ill-fated King supposedly heard his last Mass before going in to battle.

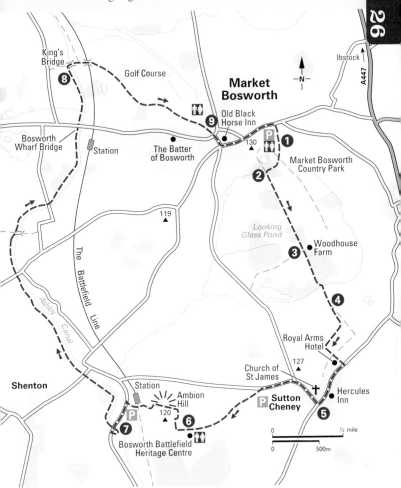

## WALK 26 DIRECTIONS

❶ Walk down the wide track from the car park to reach the children's playground and adjoining spinney, and continue across the wildflower meadow to the woods beyond. Follow the main gravel path through the trees and bear left at a fork. Look for the wide kissing gate on the left.

❷ Go through this and follow the path for just under 0.5 mile (800m) along the edge of woodland and past Looking Glass Pond.

❸ Go over a stile and on past the right of Woodhouse Farm. The path continues down along the left-hand side of a field, then crosses a stream to climb the right-hand side of the next.

**4** As the hedge falls away the well-walked path heads out across the middle of the field before turning right approaching (but not quite at) the top. It keeps to the top of the next field, then turns left across another to reach the car park of the Royal Arms Hotel. Turn right and walk through Sutton Cheney until, just past the church entrance, you turn right at the road junction (signposted 'Shenton').

**5** Follow the lane as it forks left and in 550yds (503m) turn off left through Cheney Lane car park and follow the clearly marked path across the fields to the heritage centre.

**6** Walk past the heritage centre below the car park and continue across a picnic area to a junction of paths. You can turn briefly left here to visit King Dick's Well and

the memorial to Richard III. To continue the main walk, turn right and follow the waymarked Battle Trail across Ambion Hill to reach Shenton Station. Cross the railway line by the gate and turn left out of the car park entrance on to the lane. Walk along as far as the canal bridge.

**7** Go over the bridge in order to double back and turn left beneath the bridge on to the tow path of the Ashby Canal, signposted 'Market Bosworth'.

**8** After 2.5 miles (4km) of easy and peaceful tow path walking, leave the canal at King's Bridge (No 43), the one after Bosworth Wharf Bridge. Cross this, then the railway bridge beyond for a field-edge path across stiles. This path heads half right across a golf course – aim to the left of the house in front of hilltop woodland. Go over another stile and along the top of a field before joining an unmade lane which takes you into Market Bosworth.

**9** At the end join the narrowing road (Back Lane), left and ahead, that comes out in the Market Place. Cross over and walk past The Old Black Horse Inn, then turn left into Rectory Lane. At the end of the lane is the country park.

# Flights of Fancy at Foxton Locks

*A unique staircase of locks is the focus of this pleasant walk through the South Leicestershire countryside.*

---

**DISTANCE** 5 miles (8km)   **MINIMUM TIME** 2hrs 30min

**ASCENT/GRADIENT** 213ft (65m) ▲▲▲   **LEVEL OF DIFFICULTY** ✦✦✦

**PATHS** Canal tow path and open fields (mostly pasture), 6 stiles

**LANDSCAPE** Gently rolling farmland

**SUGGESTED MAP** OS Explorer 223 Northampton & Market Harborough

**START/FINISH** Grid reference: SP 691891

**DOG FRIENDLINESS** Under control near livestock, good elsewhere (note stiles)

**PARKING** Foxton Locks long stay car park (pay-and-display)

**PUBLIC TOILETS** At car park

---

Although it might be tempting to regard Britain's canal system as an antiquated relic, a visit to the Grand Union Canal at Foxton Locks proves that it is not only still working but also remains very popular. The highlight at Foxton is a staircase of ten locks which raises the canal by 75ft (23m). It takes a boat an average of 45 minutes to negotiate all ten locks, as well as the small matter of displacing 25,000 gallons (113,650 litres) of water for the entire passage.

The locks were opened in 1814, but because they were so narrow created something of a bottleneck, and 60 years later a mechanical lift known as an 'inclined plane' was built to enable boats to be transported much more quickly. From the black-and-white photographs on show in the museum these two counterbalancing docks or tanks (which ran on rails up and down the hillside) must have been quite a spectacle, and cut the journey through Foxton down to as little as eight minutes. Unfortunately canal traffic was already waning, thanks to the competition from railway and road traffic, so the inclined plane operated for just ten years. By 1928 the equipment was sold for scrap, leaving only the grassed-over rails.

## A New Lease of Life

Today there are more boats on Britain's canals than in the commercial days, and places such as Foxton Locks are a popular visitor attraction. The fascinating Foxton Canal Museum is open daily from April to October (weekends only in winter) and is housed in the former boiler house of the inclined plane, while the pubs cater for canal traffic and tourists alike.

At the basin below the locks, a 6-mile (9.7km) arm leads to Market Harborough, although most craft head up and down the main Grand Union route. Boats can be hired, or else you can just enjoy a short afternoon cruise up and down the waterway on board *The Vagabond*. In fact, things have gone so far full circle that the Foxton Locks Partnership is even talking of restoring the site to its former glory and reintroducing the artificial lift.

Whatever your level of interest, there is something undeniably fascinating about watching a handsome and colourful narrowboat negotiate the ten

# FOXTON LOCKS

locks at Foxton. Perhaps it has something to do with the sheer ingenuity of displacing water to raise or lower a large craft, and the quiet and unhurried nature of it all. Or possibly it's simply nice to watch someone else hard at work. Either way, what can beat idling by a picturesque lock deep in the middle of the Leicestershire countryside.

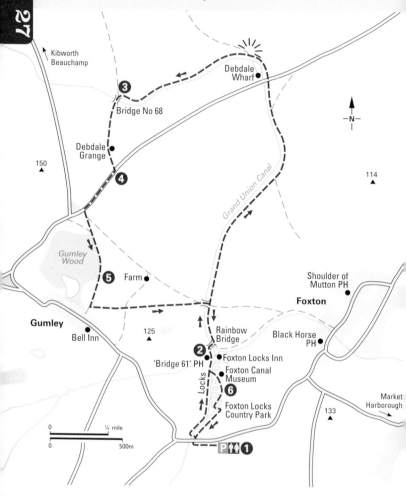

## WALK 27 DIRECTIONS

**1** Turn left out of the car park and along the signposted path parallel with the road to reach the canal. Go right, under the road bridge, then over the footbridge, in order to turn right on the far bank and along the tow path to Foxton Locks. Descend the lock staircase to reach the basin at the bottom.

**2** Go ahead past the Bridge 61 pub and switch banks via the high-arched brick footbridge (Rainbow Bridge). Walk out along the wide tow path beyond. Continue along this easy and peaceful route for 1.75 miles (2.8km), following the Grand Union Canal as it swings left beyond Debdale Wharf. Notice the large numbers of boats moored in the marina, some in preparation for repairs and renovation, while others are kept here permanently. There are lovely views over the open countryside towards Kibworth Beauchamp to the north.

**3** At bridge No 68 go over the stile on the right to cross the metal footbridge via two more stiles. On the far side make your way up the left-hand edge of a wide, sloping field to pass Debdale Grange. Continue alongside the top field to reach the lane that lies on the far side.

**4** Turn right, along the road for 0.25 mile (400m), then, approaching a road junction, go over the stile on the left for a signposted public footpath across the field. Take the right fork, aiming for the far edge of Gumley Wood – the left-hand path is signposted 'Foxton' and takes you straight back to the canal. Follow

the path closely around the side of the plantation until the second stile, beside a section of fence used as a horse jump.

**5** From here strike out across a deeply undulating grassy field towards a metal gate below trees on the far side. If you want to visit the pub in the village of Gumley, go right before the gate for a short uphill path, otherwise aim half left through the next field. Go through another gate and directly out across more fields, separated by the farm drive, to return to the canal on the very far side. Cross the high, thin footbridge and turn right to return to the basin and locks. Walk back up beside the staircase, crossing over half-way up to visit the museum.

**6** From the museum follow the popular path up along its side (don't cross the main canal again), then briefly double back to the left along a canal arm through some trees. Cross over a bridge and turn right along the tow path to return to the road bridge. Go under this and turn left to return to the car park.

*Overleaf: A colourful canal boat on Foxton Locks (Walk 27)*

# Curious Customs of Medbourne and Hallaton

*Discover some very unusual Eastertide goings-on in two picturesque South Leicestershire villages.*

**DISTANCE** *7.5 miles (12.1km)*   **MINIMUM TIME** *4hrs*

**ASCENT/GRADIENT** *787ft (240m)* ▲▲▲   **LEVEL OF DIFFICULTY** +++

**PATHS** *Farm paths, tracks, some rough and muddy, 15 stiles*

**LANDSCAPE** *Rolling pastoral scene of fields and woodland*

**SUGGESTED MAP** *OS Explorer 233 Leicester & Hinckley (224 Corby, Kettering & Wellingborough, also useful )*

**START/FINISH** *Grid reference: SP 799929*

**DOG FRIENDLINESS** *On lead near livestock beyond Hallaton (note 15 stiles)*

**PARKING** *Roadside parking near village hall, Main Street, Medbourne*

**PUBLIC TOILETS** *None on route*

Bottle-kicking, they claim in these parts, is a sport older than football, cricket and even so-called real tennis, but whether 'sport' is the right term is open to question. It takes place every Easter Monday when hundreds of people gather in Hallaton to try and propel a tiny barrel (known rather confusingly as a bottle) towards the neighbouring village of Medbourne. The villagers of Medbourne, meanwhile, try to physically stop them by any means possible. And, as far as rules go, that's about it.

But bottle-kicking is just one part of the day-long celebrations which are believed to go back to medieval times (although rather typically no-one is quite sure when). The beer inside the actual barrels plays an important part in the day's proceedings, naturally enough, as does the hare pie scrambling. The hare has long been a symbol of Easter and used to be paraded ahead of Hallaton's procession each year. Home-made hare pie is as important as the actual bottle-kicking, although the traditional dish has variously been made with beef, veal and bacon over the years. To the south of the village the walk passes Hare Pie Bank, which records show has been a local meeting place and scene of festive and religious gatherings for many centuries. This is where Easter's mayhem truly begins.

## The Order of Ceremonies

The events of Easter Monday follow a set order in Hallaton. The morning starts with the children's parade led by a marching band, after which comes the bottle-kicking service in St Michael's Church. The bottles and hare pie are then paraded through the village and the pie is cut up and 'distributed' (often thrown at the assembled mob), who move on to Hare Pie Bank to begin the contest. Like the annual Shrovetide football match at Ashbourne in Derbyshire, bottle-kicking is a rough and unruly affair, usually conducted by scrums of young men who get covered in mud and bruises. There are no set rules, no team kits, and not even any limits on numbers. The sole objective is to propel the small wooden cask to the opposing village boundary, which in Medbourne's case is several fields away over hedges and brooks. The result is usually decided from the best of three games, and afterwards the winners gather at the Butter Cross in the centre of Hallaton.

For more information on this bizarre and fascinating custom, read John Morison and Peter Daisley's engrossing book on sale at The Bewicke gift shop and tea room, behind the Bewicke Arms in Hallaton. It's also available from (and in fact published by) Hallaton Museum, on Hog Lane, open weekend afternoons and bank holidays from Easter to October.

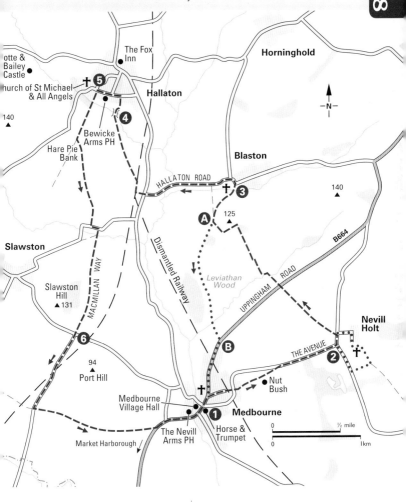

## WALK 28 DIRECTIONS

❶ Walk up Main Street and turn right on to Rectory Lane, opposite the church, which becomes a path. Go over the road at the end and up through the fields opposite. Cross a stile to continue through the yard of Nut Bush and across the field beyond, then climb over

the low wall on your left to the road. Turn right and walk along the road to reach Nevill Holt.

❷ Turn left at the end and, where the brick wall finishes go, left through a gate to cross a wide arable field. Go through a gate and drop down through two fields, separated by Uppingham Road.

Beyond a woodland strip go left, then up the right-hand side and across the top of the next field – aim for the solitary tree on the skyline. At the far corner drop down to the right to join a track. Turn right when you reach a junction (Point **A**) and walk the farm track into Blaston.

**3** At the lovely Church of St Giles turn left and follow Hallaton Road to the junction at the end. Go straight over and after the second stile turn right to walk through open pasture towards Hallaton. Follow the yellow-topped waymark posts, aiming initially for the spire of Hallaton church, then veer to the right of an isolated clump of trees in the middle of the field, and cross a footbridge.

## WHAT TO LOOK FOR

The Parish Church of St Michael and All Angels at Hallaton has historic links with St Morrell, a French monk (St Maurille) who became the Bishop of Angers in the Loire Valley. It's thought that Norman settlers at Hallaton may have established a chapel dedicated to the saint, and over the centuries a local cult developed in the area.

**4** Go left, then sharply right beyond a stile and follow the signs through a small, modern housing development. Eventually turn left on to Medbourne Road and straight on to reach the centre of Hallaton.

## WHERE TO EAT AND DRINK

There are three excellent pubs, which all serve food daily: The Nevill Arms at Medbourne, and the Bewicke Arms and Fox Inn at Hallaton. The Nevill Arms is situated beside a stream at the start of the walk, while the Fox Inn overlooks the pretty village pond at Hallaton. The Bewicke tea room, behind the Bewicke Arms, is open daily. There is also the Horse & Trumpet, a restaurant in an old pub opposite the church at Medbourne.

**5** Leave the village via a passageway underneath a house, just along from the Bewicke Arms and almost opposite the Butter Cross. Cross a footbridge and go directly up a sloping field, aiming just to the right of a wooden fence beneath trees. Arriving at the summit of Hare Pie Bank, go through a gate and turn left on to a wide track (part of the Macmillan Way, a route running from Lincolnshire to Dorset specially created to raise funds for the Macmillan Cancer Relief charity). Continue along the edge of two gated fields, then turn left into a lane. Turn right at the first bend and follow this long, semi-surfaced lane below Slawston Hill.

**6** At a road junction go straight over and down a lane, and 500yds (457m) beyond the former railway bridge turn left for an unswerving bridleway along the foot of successive fields. When you reach the far end, turn left to follow the road back into Medbourne.

## WHILE YOU'RE THERE

Just to the west of Hallaton village is a motte-and-bailey castle, visible from the nearby lane or public footpath. Introduced by the Normans (the Anglo Saxons were not great castle builders) the 'motte' was a flat-topped conical mound of earth, usually topped by a wooden palisade and tower, located either inside or next to an embanked enclosure known as the 'bailey'. Stone-built fortresses eventually superseded these earth-and-timber defences.

# A Gentler Medbourne Circuit

*This shorter route omits Hallaton, but allows you to spend some time exploring Nevill Holt's fine period buildings.*
**See map and information panel for Walk 28**

> **DISTANCE** *3.75 miles (6km)* **MINIMUM TIME** *2hrs*
> **ASCENT/GRADIENT** *426ft (130m)* ▲▲▲ **LEVEL OF DIFFICULTY** ✦✦✦

## WALK 29 DIRECTIONS
### (Walk 28 option)

Approaching Nevill Holt from Medbourne on the main walk you pass through a grand gateway next to the intriguingly named Buffalo Lodge. Ahead is a wide, double-tree-lined thoroughfare called 'The Avenue'. So what is at the end of all this?

The answer is an impressive medieval manor house established by Thomas Palmer, and later developed by his successors, the Nevills, in the early 1400s. Palmer received a royal licence to 'impark' 300 acres (121ha) of arable land after the village of a dozen or so families was deserted at about that time (see Walk 41 for more details on this subject).

Between 1876 and 1912 it was owned by the Cunard family, the famous shipping magnates, and an inscription above the bay window of Buffalo Lodge reads 'BC 1880' after Sir Bache Cunard. The house was used until recently as a school, but is now a private home. In its grounds is the 13th-century church containing alabaster and black marble tombs of Nevill family members.

Turn right at the end of The Avenue to walk past the ornate gates, then take the path across parkland to the south of the site which loops back towards the church. From here a public road, via estate cottages and the edge of a high brick wall, leads back to the main route at Point ❷.

For the short route back to Medbourne leave Walk 28 at Point Ⓐ. Where the main route turns right for the village of Blaston turn left, on a wide farm track, and follow this obvious and easy route past a copse and down through open farmland. On your right towards the foot of the hill is Leviathan Wood, planted in 2005 by the Woodland Trust to commemorate the 200th anniversary of the Battle of Trafalgar. The path crosses a brook, passes some farm buildings on the left, then reaches Uppingham Road (Point Ⓑ).

Turn right, back into Medbourne, crossing the bridge over the former railway as you do so.

# Prehistoric Burrough Hill

*This short walk to an ancient Leicestershire hilltop is rich in atmosphere.*

---

**DISTANCE** 3.5 miles (5.7km)  **MINIMUM TIME** 1hr 30min

**ASCENT/GRADIENT** 295ft (90m) ▲▲▲  **LEVEL OF DIFFICULTY** ✦✦✦

**PATHS** Variety of field paths and tracks, some steep slopes

**LANDSCAPE** Low rolling hills and patchwork farmland

**SUGGESTED MAP** OS Explorer 246 Loughborough

**START/FINISH** Grid reference: SK 766115

**DOG FRIENDLINESS** Under tight control near livestock on Burrough Hil

**PARKING** Pay-and-display car park at Burrough Hill

**PUBLIC TOILETS** At car park

---

## WALK 30 DIRECTIONS

Since 1970 Leicestershire County Council has managed the distinctive and popular summit of Burrough Hill as a Country Park, and access is via the official car park off the road between Burrough on the Hill and Somerby.

Walk out of the car park along the wide gated track to the earthworks that crown the summit of the hill. Head right, towards the trig point, and go around the grassy ramparts in an anti-clockwise direction. At the far side is a handy toposcope identifying what you can see – and what you can't. Apparently Boston Stump is 41 miles (66km) distant, but you'll need an exceptionally clear day to make it out.

At 690ft (210m) Burrough Hill is one of the highest points in Leicestershire and commands excellent views in virtually every direction. The earthworks are thought to date from the last few centuries BC, and the deep ditch and broad embankments, probably topped by a high wooden fence,

were likely used as a place of refuge for local settlers and their livestock in times of attack from other tribes. Some Roman coins and fragments of pottery have been found, and a stretch of cobbled surface and the foundations of what might have been a guard house were unearthed near the main entrance to the fort. However, since no detailed archaeological research has been carried out, the precise history of the site is still unclear – but perhaps that's not such a bad thing after all. The absence of modern interpretation boards at every turn encourages us to use our imaginations, and envisage the situation as it might have been 2,000 years ago.

### WHILE YOU'RE THERE

When the Parish Brewery at Burrough on the Hill began life in 1983, it was one of the first in the East Midlands to brew its own beer. It has an entry in the *Guinness Book of Records* for brewing what it claims is the strongest beer in the world with an ABV (alcohol by volume) of a leg-wobbling 23 per cent.

WALK 30

Continue all the way around the embankment, until you're facing the gate you entered by, and here drop down the wide, stone-filled track to the right. This swings gently around and below the western edge of the hill, with the toposcope above. At the end go through two gates for a wide path around the field ahead.

> ## WHAT TO LOOK FOR
> Burrough Hill sits on an outcrop of marlstone, a band of ironstone whose distinctive warming colours can be found in local cottages, barns and churches. It forms many of the other prominent hilltop locations in this area too.

Follow this across to the far side, but before you reach the lane go through a gap in the hedge on the right for a short path, clearly indicated, across the adjoining field. Look back at the hill behind you and see how prominent and imposing it appears. Imagine it topped with a forbidding wooden palisade, and wild, bearded men waving spears and yelling at you from behind. Still fancy attacking?

Go through another gap in the hedge and turn right, into the lane, and walk this for 0.5 mile (800m), going straight on at the junction (signposted 'Little Dalby'). Follow the lane as it swings right at Moscow Farm, opposite a row of handsome brick sheds.

Approximately 420yds (384m) beyond the farm is a stile in the hedge to the right. Indicated 'public footpath', it leads along the right-hand edge of a rising field and then through undergrowth to the left of a small area of woodland called Burrough Hill Covert. However, the first 50yds (46m) beyond the stile can get quite overgrown in the height of summer, and if this is the case continue along the lane for a further 100yds (91m) and turn right on to an unsigned farm track. This public access route follows the left-hand edge of the field and makes its way gradually up the hill, steepening towards the top where the woods close in. The presence of a small spring, and the attentions of horse-riders and cyclists, can make the upper section a bit boggy. The aforementioned footpath joins from the right just before a set of double gates. Go through these and continue up and along the grassy path straight ahead, following the bottom of a small valley.

The ancient defences are high above to your right. Do you think you can make it up the steep banks without being seen and enter the stronghold? (And will you have any puff left when you get there?)

> ## WHERE TO EAT AND DRINK
> The Stag and Hounds at Burrough on the Hill, The Royal Oak at Great Dalby, and The Stilton Cheese Inn at Somerby all welcome children, have outdoor seating, and serve food daily.

When you reach the very top turn right and either follow the yellow-painted posts across the pasture for the main gate and the track back to the car park, or wander back over to the ramparts once more. In modern times the hilltop was the scene of various meetings and festivities, including sports events and hunting. In the 19th century the Somerby and Burrough Hill race meetings were held here, with crowds of spectators lining the ramparts to watch the horses being ridden around in the arena below.

# Villages of the Wreake

*A gentle wander through North Leicestershire's little-known Wreake Valley.*

---

**DISTANCE** 3.75 miles (6km)   **MINIMUM TIME** 1hr 45min

**ASCENT/GRADIENT** 150ft (40m) ▲▲▲   **LEVEL OF DIFFICULTY** ✦✦✦

**PATHS** Pasture, ploughed fields heavy if wet, 14 stiles

**LANDSCAPE** Gentle, open river valley of fields and woodland

**SUGGESTED MAP** OS Explorer 246 Loughborough

**START/FINISH** Grid reference: SK 694176

**DOG FRIENDLINESS** Under close control around livestock, heavy stile count

**PARKING** Roadside parking on Main Street or Water Street, Frisby

**PUBLIC TOILETS** None on route (nearest in Melton Mowbray)

---

The valley of the Wreake, west of Melton Mowbray, is a broad, low affair, whose rather meandering and dilatory river reflects the quiet and unhurried villages that line its route. Indeed, the name Wreake is believed to derive from an Old Norse word meaning twisted, probably given to it by early Danish settlers. Likewise Frisby's equally engaging village name has nothing to do with wacky playthings that you may remember from your childhood days, but instead is derived from the Frisians, who came from the other side of the North Sea to make their way up the Trent and Soar rivers before setting up camp in the Wreake Valley.

Frisby is a charming and handsome place, with a collection of fascinating period buildings including thatch and brick (and painted brick), as well as a little traditional ironstone, most notably the church. It's as pleasant on the eye as the well-kept pint of local ale at The Bell Inn is on the palate.

The old and rather battered-looking stone cross at the junction of Main Street and Water Street was originally a preaching cross, used by the Cistercian monks from nearby Launde Abbey, and later became a market cross. Latterly it's been moved back from the roadside after a few close calls with today's uncompromising traffic. Just along from here is Zion House, a thatched building dating from 1725, and once the home of a well-known highwayman. But he robbed one mail coach too many, and was hanged at Birstall, near Leicester, in 1797.

## A Tale of Two Churches

The most notorious vicar of Frisby's Church of St Thomas of Canterbury was Revd William Wragge. In the 1700s he turned Frisby into a short-lived Gretna Green by marrying couples without bothering to read the banns, and when he was finally apprehended and sentenced to transportation he pleaded old age and was let off scot-free.

St Thomas's neat and well-tended graveyard is matched by that of St Peter's at Kirby Bellars, further along the route, whose now sealed-up vaults were once the final resting place of various local knights. The village name partly derives from lord of the manor Roger de Beler, who founded

# FRISBY ON THE WREAKE

a chapel in the church for priests, and in 1319 was granted permission to build an adjacent Augustinian priory. But this created local conflict and Roger was murdered by feuding family members a short time later. Dissolution in the 16th century meant the end of the priory, and all that remains today are some rough earthworks in a field north of the church. Fourteenth-century effigies of the murdered Roger de Beler and his wife can be seen in the south aisle of the church.

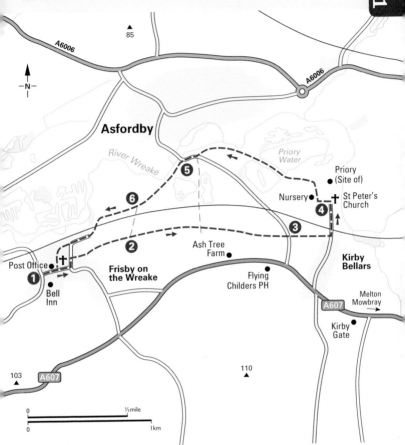

## WALK 31 DIRECTIONS

❶ Walk eastwards along Frisby's Main Street, past the post office, and turn left into Mill Lane. After 50yds (46m) turn right between houses on a public footpath (denoted by a fingerpost bearing a footprint). Walk out across an open field, dropping slightly downhill, then go through a double gate and ahead through the second field.

❷ Ignore the turning down to the railway (left), but instead continue across further wide fields, with Ash Tree Farm away to your right. Despite the lack of a well-walked path the route is clearly indicated by a succession of yellow-topped signposts, until you arrive finally at a road.

❸ Go across and continue through two smaller fields, the second in which horses are usually kept, and via the kissing gate in the corner to reach the houses of Kirby Bellars. Turn left and walk down the lane to the church.

❹ Continue down the narrowing lane, which twists left, then right, past a nursery. The track emerges into an open field where you should turn left and follow the clear path across the meadow. Go over a stile by a lifebuoy for a leafy

path along the causeway across Priory Water, former gravel pits now run as a nature reserve. At the end go ahead over more stiles, as the path veers left and follows the bank of the River Wreake. It then winds its way through a copse to end at the road bridge into Asfordby.

❺ If you want to visit Asfordby turn right and take the surfaced pathway off to the right on the far side of the bridge. Otherwise cross the road (but not the bridge) for the path opposite, which initially shadows the river then strikes out diagonally left across two fields. Aim for the far corner of the second, with the spire of Frisby church just in view above the treetops ahead of you.

❻ Turn right and walk along a narrow, grassy field parallel with the railway, then negotiate the railway via the pedestrian crossing. Follow the lane on the far side until it bends left. Here go right into Carrfields Lane, then left via a short alleyway and another quiet back street to reach Church Lane. Turn left and follow this back to the Main Street. The entrance to the church is via the side of the old school building.

# A Rutland Waterside Walk

*A short, but scenic, introduction to the aquatic charms of Rutland Water.*

---

**DISTANCE** *4.5 miles (7.2km)*   **MINIMUM TIME** *2hrs*

**ASCENT/GRADIENT** *311ft (95m)* ▲▲▲   **LEVEL OF DIFFICULTY** ✦✦✦

**PATHS** *Wide and firm the whole distance, 3 stiles*

**LANDSCAPE** *Low-lying peninsula of dipping fields and woodland*

**SUGGESTED MAP** *OS Explorer 234 Rutland Water*

**START/FINISH** *Grid reference: SK 900075*

**DOG FRIENDLINESS** *On lead in fields of stock and around nesting birds*

**PARKING** *Roadside parking in Hambleton*

**PUBLIC TOILETS** *None on route (nearest in Oakham)*

---

That England's smallest county contains its biggest stretch of inland water is impressive enough, but in fact Rutland Water's beautifully designed 3,100 acres (1,255ha) also make it one of the largest artificial lakes in the whole of Western Europe.

Work began in 1973 with the flooding of the Gwash Valley and abandonment of the two villages of Nether and Middle Hambleton, leaving Upper Hambleton (now simply called Hambleton) virtually marooned on an island in the middle of the lake. Although the reservoir was created in order to supply drinking water, Rutland Water has become a busy destination for outdoor pursuits. Sailing and windsurfing are very popular, while fishermen are to be found on the shores and out in boats in virtually all weathers. There are picnic sites along the northern edge, a museum at the preserved church at Normanton on the southern shore, and afternoon cruises on the *Rutland Belle* that plies the water daily between May and September. A 25-mile (40km) off-road cycling route encompasses the whole of Rutland Water, and cycle hire is available at Whitwell and Normanton in the summer months.

## An Ornithological Feast

The nature reserve at the far western end of Rutland Water is managed by Leicestershire and Rutland Wildlife Trust, and your first port of call should be the Anglian Water Bird Watching Centre at Egleton. From here you can obtain a permit to walk to the 20 different hides that are dotted around the secluded bays and artificially created lagoons, or go on to visit Lyndon Nature Reserve on the southern side of Manton Bay. Rutland Water is one of the most important centres for wildfowl in Britain – as many as 23,500 ducks have been recorded on a single winter's day, and a total of 250 different species of birds have been seen since 1975.

Ducks such as pochard, teal, gadwall and shoveler are a common sight around Rutland Water, while waders like redshank and sandpipers are frequent visitors. An hour or two in a hide and your list will probably include terns, lapwing, cormorants, grebes, and so on, plus perhaps a few more unusual sightings such as a merganser or a godwit.

# RUTLAND WATER

However, there is one rare fish-eating bird that has had the birders fumbling at their binocular cases over the past few years. In 1996 a programme was initiated to translocate young osprey chicks from Scotland to Rutland, and since then several of these majestic birds of prey have returned from their hazardous African migration to set up home at Rutland – the first time ospreys have nested in England in more than 150 years. However, the long-term fate of the Rutland ospreys is far from secure, since the birds mate for life and have very few chicks, but with careful protection and gentle encouragement the outlook for the so-called fish eagles is hopeful.

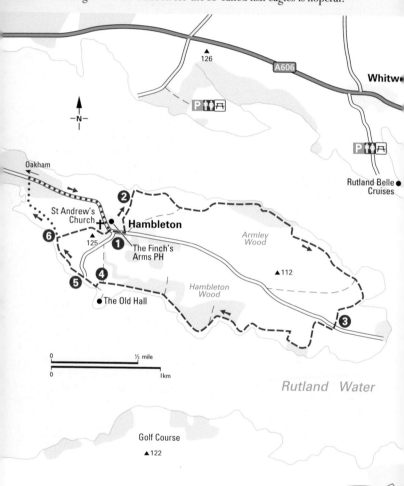

## WALK 32 DIRECTIONS

**1** From St Andrew's Church in the centre of Hambleton, walk eastwards on the long main street as far as the red pillar box. Turn left opposite the pillar box on a wide track indicated 'public

footpath' that leads straight through a gate and down the middle of a sloping field.

**2** Go through the gate at the bottom of the field and turn right on to the wide track that runs just above the shore. This popular and peaceful route around the Hambleton peninsula is shared with cyclists, so enjoy the walk, but be alert. Follow it from field to field, and through Armley Wood, with ever-changing views across Rutland Water. As you gradually swing around the tip of the Hambleton peninsula with views towards the dam at the eastern end, you can begin to appreciate the sheer size of the reservoir, and how the birds, anglers, sailors and other users can all happily co-exist.

**3** When you arrive at a tarmac lane (which is gated to traffic at this point, since it simply disappears into the water a little further on!), go straight across to continue on the same unmade track. It turns right and runs parallel with the road a short distance, before heading left and back towards the peaceful water's edge and a lovely section of mixed woodland. Continue along the lakeside for just over 1 mile (1.6km).

---

**WHERE TO EAT AND DRINK**

The Finch's Arms at Hambleton is an elegant public house where the emphasis is on high-quality bar food and restaurant meals, and from the back terrace there are great views out across the northern sweep of Rutland Water. Booking is advisable for peak times. A full range of cafés and pubs is to be found in Oakham, 3 miles (4.8km) away.

---

**4** Approaching The Old Hall, a handsome building perched just above the shore, turn left to reach its surfaced drive, then go right and walk along it for 160yds (146m) to reach a cattle grid.

**5** At this point you can return directly to Hambleton by following the lane back uphill;

---

**WHILE YOU'RE THERE**

Just to the south of Rutland Water is the picturesque village of Wing, where apart from two decent pubs there is a most unusual and historic maze. Cut into the roadside turf near the recreation ground, Wing Maze is based on an 11-ringed design often found on the floors of medieval French cathedrals.
Wing itself once had a monastery, and it's possible that the monks may have followed the lines of the maze, stopping to pray at certain points.

---

otherwise veer left to continue along the open, waterside track, with views across to Egleton Bay and the corner of Rutland Water specially reserved for wildlife (it's out of bounds to sailing boats).

**6** After about 500yds (457m) look for the easily missed stile in the hedge on your right, and the public footpath that heads straight up the field. (If you overshoot, or want to extend the walk by 0.5 mile (800m), simply carry on along the track to the very far end and return along the lane to the village.) Aim for the apex of the field, where successive stiles lead to a narrow passageway between a hedge and a fence that eventually brings you out in the churchyard in the centre of the village.

---

**WHAT TO LOOK FOR**

It's said that there's no higher land between Upper Hambleton and the Wash and, although modest in height, the hilltop position of the village of course spared it from the watery fate that claimed its neighbours. Among the views from the peninsula is Burley on the Hill, a striking mansion on a densely wooded ridge to the north that was built for David Finch, Earl of Nottingham, between 1694 and 1705.

# The Miniature Charm of Rutland

*Explore the open countryside and parkland around Exton,
a thatched village north of Rutland Water.*

---

**DISTANCE** 6.5 miles (10.4km)   **MINIMUM TIME** 3hrs

**ASCENT/GRADIENT** 425ft (130m) ▲▲▲   **LEVEL OF DIFFICULTY** ✦✦✦

**PATHS** *Mainly field paths and firm farm tracks, 10 stiles*

**LANDSCAPE** *Open and undulating fields and parkland, mixed woodland*

**SUGGESTED MAP** *OS Explorer 234 Rutland Water*

**START/FINISH** *Grid reference: SK 924112*

**DOG FRIENDLINESS** *On lead near livestock, beware awkward stiles*

**PARKING** *Roadside parking on The Green, Exton*

**PUBLIC TOILETS** *None on route (nearest at Barnsdale Gardens)*

---

Located a couple of miles north of Rutland Water, Exton is a picturesque village of ironstone and thatched cottages laid out around a green ringed by mature sycamore trees and overlooked by the attractive, tall, creeper-covered village pub.

There has been a community here since Norman times, and once the manor belonged to King David of Scotland. Since then it has changed hands a number of times, finally passing to the Noels, Viscounts Campden, Earls of Gainsborough, in the 1620s. The family still owns neighbouring Exton Hall, which was built to replace the Old Hall after it was largely destroyed by a fire in 1810. The ruins of the Old Hall are inside the grounds (accessible to the public from the road to the south) close to the Church of St Peter and St Paul, which itself was struck by lightning in 1843, causing the spire to collapse. Despite some of the original work being lost, most of the fine monuments survived, including some medieval sculptures and various tombs. Also look out for the giant memorial by the master carver Grinling Gibbons to the 3rd Viscount Campden, his fourth wife and 19 children, which is considered something of a rarity since Gibbons is far better known for working in wood rather than stone. The film *Little Lord Fauntleroy* (1980) was shot on location in Exton and featured, among other places, the village church.

## Exton's Glorious Grounds

The grounds and parkland were mainly developed in the late 17th century by the 6th Earl of Gainsborough, when water features, such as cascades, artificial ponds and streams, were created (proving that landscaper gardeners were at it 300 years before any television makeover show you could mention). Among the ornamental follies on the estate is an elaborate Gothic summer house that dates from the late 18th century. It is known as Fort Henry, and overlooks Fort Henry Lake, which you will see half-way round the walk. Behind it, until quite recently, stood the even more bizarre Bark Temple, an elaborate wooden structure that not surprisingly has rotted away over time.

# EXTON

## Rutland: a County in Miniature

Measuring less than 20 miles (32.4km) across, Rutland has a resident population of around 37,000, and apart from Oakham and Uppingham most of its inhabitants live in tiny villages and hamlets like Exton. The county's name possibly derives from the 11th-century word 'Roteland', denoting the red colour of the soil in the east of the region; or it could have been part of the estate belonging to an early landowner called Rota. For many years this tiny place was in the hands of either the Crown or the Church, but in 1974 local government reorganisation ended its independence and relegated it to a mere district of Leicestershire. Happily that decision was reversed in 1997, and Rutland is once more England's smallest county, whose Latin motto *Multum in Parvo* means 'so much in so little'.

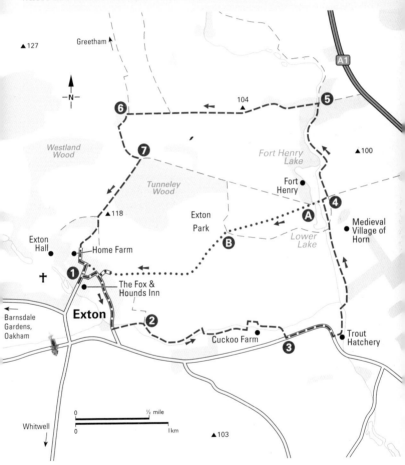

## WALK 33 DIRECTIONS

❶ With your back to the pub leave The Green on the far right-hand side on Stamford Road and, at the end, turn right. This becomes Empingham Road and, when the houses finish, continue over the stream and go over a stile on your left to follow a public footpath.

❷ Just before a gate at the entrance to a field, bear right to follow a wide, grassy track along the shallow valley, keeping the stream to your right. Stay on this track for just under 1 mile (1.6km), at one point crossing the stream and returning via a footbridge before climbing into a field on the left to avoid Cuckoo Farm. Finally the path crosses the stream once more and clambers up through the fields on the right to reach a lane.

**3** Turn left and walk along the verge until just beyond the bend, then go left on a footpath indicated 'Fort Henry and Greetham'. Follow this route above the trout hatchery, then head diagonally right via a small concrete bridge to reach the fence at the top. Turn left and walk along to Lower Lake, then go ahead on the surfaced drive for a few paces, to fork left before the gate and head out across open pasture above the water.

### WHILE YOU'RE THERE
Barnsdale Gardens, a mile (1.6km) west of Exton, will be familiar to millions of TV gardeners as the home of the late Geoff Hamilton. Open to the public daily, there are 37 gardens within the south-facing 8-acre (3.2ha) site, plus an arboretum, coffee shop and a well-stocked nursery with a range of garden plants initially propagated from the gardens.

**4** At the far side turn right on to another lane then, in a few paces, left for the footpath indicated 'Greetham'. Follow this beside Fort Henry Lake, then on along a corridor between lovely mixed woodland. At the far end climb the stairs to reach the lane.

**5** Turn left and walk up through more woods and, when the semi-surfaced drive bears left, go straight on through an area of newly planted trees. The wide,

### WHAT TO LOOK FOR
Although the gentle farmland of Rutland and South Lincolnshire is by and large a peaceful place and makes for restful walking, every now and then you may be aware of a distant roar and a fast-moving object zooming through the sky. A few miles to the north lies the busy airfield at Cottesmore, which opened in 1938 and was a base for American bombers throughout the Second World War. Today it is used for the training of Tornado pilots.

unmade track now heads directly out across the open fields for a mile (1.6km).

**6** When you reach the trees on the far side turn left on to a track that drops down and bears left. Here go straight on via a stile and wooden plank footbridge and head up diagonally left towards the top of the field. Go over the stile and turn left on to the farm track once more.

### WHERE TO EAT AND DRINK
The Fox and Hounds Inn by The Green in Exton is an elegant 17th-century pub which serves food daily (except Monday) and has a pleasant garden situated to the rear. Alternatively visit the coffee shop at Barnsdale Gardens (see While You're There), which is open all year round (closed Monday and Tuesday from November to February).

**7** At the junction turn right on to the straight, metalled lane, signposted 'Viking Way to Exton'. Bear left at a fork before woods and follow this back to Exton. Follow signs around Home Farm, then follow West End round to the left and turn right by the stone shelter into High Street to return to The Green.

# Exton's Modest Heights

*A short cut to Exton allowing wide views over Rutland.*
**See map and information panel for Walk 33**

---

**DISTANCE** 5 miles (8km)   **MINIMUM TIME** 2hrs 30min
**ASCENT/GRADIENT** 393ft (120m) ▲▲▲   **LEVEL OF DIFFICULTY** +++

---

## WALK 34 DIRECTIONS (Walk 33 option)

Leave Walk 33 at Point **4**, where it reaches a surfaced lane that bisects Fort Henry Lake and Lower Lake. Turn left and walk uphill until it veers right (Point **A**). Here go straight on, over a stone-filled patch of ground, for a rough grassy track that heads through some newly planted trees and out, straight ahead across the open hilltop.

The vast, hedgeless fields stretch out in all directions, and from the top of this small and sometimes windy plateau there are views across the Rutland countryside. In the distance ahead is the dense green woodland surrounding Exton Hall, while closer to hand is Tunneley Wood. Together with the intensive farmland you are walking across, this is all part of the Exton Estate. Don't forget, however, that it's private land, so stick to the well-signposted public rights of way.

The dips in some of the fields, especially to the north, are the result of former ironstone workings. The ironstone outcrop forms a low ridge that runs across Northamptonshire, Leicestershire and Rutland and produces distinctive chestnut or orange/brown soils. Since medieval times the shallow quarries have provided stone for local buildings and, although long exhausted, they have resulted in a series of peculiarly low or uneven fields.

When the grassy track dips down to reach a junction of routes (Point **B**), go straight across, indicated 'public bridleway'. Walk along this open surfaced lane as it gradually climbs up towards Exton, approaching the village along a slender avenue of trees. Go through the gate and continue along New Field Road past houses. At the end turn right (look out for the millennium walnut tree on an open patch of grass) and walk along Stamford Road into Top Street. Go left by the stone shelter into High Street and past a row of beautiful thatched cottages in order to return to the pub on The Green.

### WHAT TO LOOK FOR

Just below Lower Lake is the moated outline of a former trout pool, fish pond or possibly a stockade of some sort. It was probably built at the same time as the now deserted medieval village of Horn, whose buildings once stood on the hillside above North Brook and today remain as simple, grassy outlines.

# Stamford's Architecture

*Discover historic Stamford, one of the finest 'stone towns' in England.*

| | |
|---|---|
| **DISTANCE** 2.5 miles (4km) | **MINIMUM TIME** 1hr 30min |
| **ASCENT/GRADIENT** 188ft (55m) ▲▲▲ | **LEVEL OF DIFFICULTY** +++ |

**PATHS** Surfaced paths and pavements
**LANDSCAPE** Churches and squares, narrow alleyways and historic inns
**SUGGESTED MAP** OS Explorer 234 Rutland Water
**START/FINISH** Grid reference: TF 030072
**DOG FRIENDLINESS** Good in The Meadows, use poop scoop bins
**PARKING** Car parks around town, including North Street (pay-and-display)
**PUBLIC TOILETS** Red Lion Square and Stamford Arts Centre

## WALK 35 DIRECTIONS

The walk starts at Stamford Museum (free admission, closed Sunday) on Broad Street. Leaving the entrance turn left and walk along Broad Street. Ahead, across the road, is Browne's Hospital, established as an almshouse in the late 15th century by a wealthy local wool merchant.

Founded in Saxon times, Stamford was already a prosperous centre by the early 1300s thanks to the export of wool and cloth, attracting religious orders and academics. Today there is an engaging mix of buildings, from medieval churches and almshouses through to fine Georgian town houses and public buildings like the theatre, assembly rooms and library, and because the town was designated a conservation area in 1967 it has been spared from unsightly modern development. The low, balanced skyline is punctuated by church spires and clumps of trees, and because most of the town's foremost buildings are made from locally quarried limestone they exude a natural mellow colour complemented by the famous Collyweston roof slates, each size still bearing a different name. Stamford's well-preserved streets have been used in several period TV productions, including the BBC adaptation of George Eliot's *Middlemarch*.

Turn left into Ironmonger Street and, at the end, go right into the High Street (pedestrians only). At the end is Red Lion Square, which is dominated by the soaring spires and towers of churches. On your left is St John the Baptist, whose nave and chancel roof are lined with rows of wooden angels; while to your right is the equally imposing All Saints, described as 'the hub of Stamford' by Nikolaus Pevsner.

### WHERE TO EAT AND DRINK

There are numerous cafés, pubs and restaurants all around the town including the café at Stamford Arts Centre, the pub at All Saints Brewery, and the George Hotel on High Street St Martin's.

Turn right and walk on to and up the (initially cobbled) Barn Hill, passing a number of impressive town houses. One of these, Stukeley House, was the home of the antiquarian William Stukeley. At the end bear round to the left and, emerging on Scotgate, turn left opposite the pointed gables and terracotta of Truesdale Hospital to return to Red Lion Square. Bear round to the right and into All Saints' Street, past the restored steam-operated brewery, established in 1825, which now specialises in fruit beers.

---

**WHAT TO LOOK FOR**

Among the fascinating exhibits at Stamford Museum is a display on the life of 52-stone (330kg) Daniel Lambert, commonly regarded as England's largest man. He was born in Leicester in 1770 and, after a short spell as a jail-keeper, he died in a Stamford pub during a visit to the races at the age of 39.

---

When you reach Kings Mill Lane, turn left and drop down this cobbled thoroughfare, coming out into Bath Row. Once past the former public bathhouse turn right for a path that crosses The Meadows, a grassy strip by the River Welland. If you fancy stretching your legs a little further, a public footpath provides a riverside route upstream for 1 mile (1.6km) or so.

On the far side of the second footbridge turn left into Station Road and, passing the Burghley Almshouses, turn right into High Street St Martin's by the George Hotel. This famous old coaching inn, which stands on the former Great North Road (the equivalent of today's M1 or A1), reflects the town's renaissance in the late 18th to early 19th century as a stop-off

point on the main stagecoach route between London and York. Passengers waited in the oak-panelled London Room near the entrance and, as the sign proudly declares, at least three kings and many other famous travellers have stayed here over the years. The gallows or scaffold sign that spans the road outside the George is one of only a handful still remaining in the country, and was occasionally used as a gibbet for luckless highway robbers.

Turn left into Barnack Road, and walk along until you draw level with the pedestrian entrance to Burghley Park. Turn left and walk down Water Street and, after rounding the corner by the grand former station building, cross the river on your right via Albert Bridge. Go along Albert Road, then cross Wharf Road via the zebra crossing to go half left into Blackfriars Street in order to reach St George's Square. At the far side Stamford Arts Centre incorporates the tourist information centre. Turn right and go up Maiden Lane and, at the top of this turn right, at the end of the High Street opposite the public library, and out along St Paul's Street. At one point Stamford Boys School occupies both sides of the road, and on an old doorway at the end by the traffic lights is the Brasenose Knocker which, as a notice explains, was presented by the Oxford college to commemorate Stamford's early attempt to rival Oxford as a university town.

Cross the road and return on the far pavement to turn right into Star Lane, which then leads back to Broad Street and the museum.

# It All Comes Out in The Wash

*Choose between a wildlife wander or a spectacular aircraft display on the South Lincolnshire coast.*

DISTANCE 5.75 *miles (9.2km)*   MINIMUM TIME *2hrs 30min*

ASCENT/GRADIENT *Negligible* ▲▲▲   LEVEL OF DIFFICULTY ✦✦✦

PATHS *Field-edges, firm tracks and sea banks, 1 stile*

LANDSCAPE *Open arable fields and bare marsh and mudflats*

SUGGESTED MAP *OS Explorer 249 Spalding & Holbeach*

START/FINISH *Grid reference: TF 463292*

DOG FRIENDLINESS *Overhead military planes on weekdays can be very loud*

PARKING *Roadside parking in centre of Gedney Drove End (off A17 east of Holbeach)*

PUBLIC TOILETS *None on route*

It has to be said that the Wash is a peculiar sort of place. On the Norfolk side is Hunstanton, England's only east coast resort where you can watch the sun setting across the water (it faces west). The rivers Welland, Witham, Nene and Great Ouse all issue out into this vast shallow lagoon covering 300 square miles (776sq km), which is sometimes covered by water but more often than not by endless tidal mudflats. These have built up over a long period as the four rivers have deposited huge quantities of clay and silt. The various burrowing and surface invertebrates here have attracted a healthy bird population. In fact the Wash supports more birds than any other estuary in Britain, plus one of Europe's largest concentrations of common seals, and comprises England's largest national nature reserve.

## Pushing Back the Sea

Much of the walking around the edge of the Wash is along high embankments, which mark more than 300 years' of reclaiming farmland from the sea. This particular route around Gedney Drove End follows both the old and the current sea bank, which as you will see has allowed the rich agricultural belt to be extended right up to the sea wall. Dykes and drainage channels, controlled by sluices and pumping stations continue to keep the salt water at bay and maintain this artificially fertile land.

## Target Practice

A number of military airfields dot the Lincolnshire coast, and planes from nearby RAF Holbeach in particular use a range off the Gedney coast for bombing practice. As you walk along the sea bank, past a number of official observation towers, the small but brightly coloured targets are scattered offshore across the salt marsh. Red flags fly all along the shore when bombing is taking place (weekdays between 9am and 5pm), but it is safe and legal to walk along the sea bank and watch the proceedings (as indeed many people do), as long as you obey official signs and don't venture beyond the sea wall or pick up any unusual-looking souvenirs from the ground.

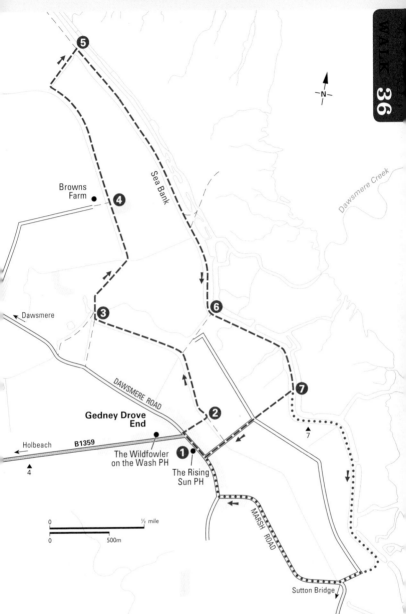

## WALK 36 DIRECTIONS

❶ With your back to The Rising Sun pub, turn left and walk along Dawsmere Road past the junction and take the signposted public footpath on the right, between bungalows, opposite the playground sign. At the far side of the field go across a small footbridge and up some steps in order to turn left into a wide field.

❷ For 1 mile (1.6km) walk along the edge of this field, which is in fact the line of the former sea

**WALK 36**

wall, keeping more or less parallel with the present and much higher sea bank over to your right. And as a sign indicates, continue straight ahead at the point where the old sea bank veers invitingly away to the right.

❸ When the field eventually ends near a strip of woodland turn right for 50yds (46m) then, faced with a small thicket, drop down to join the wide farm track on your left. Turn right, and follow the main, higher route (ignore the lower track) alongside a narrow shelter-belt of woodland which includes apple, cherry, hazel and birch. This wide, gravel track heads out towards the sea bank then bends left and continues past Browns Farm.

### WHERE TO EAT AND DRINK

The Rising Sun in Gedney Drove End welcomes families, has a beer garden to the rear, and hot and cold food is served every lunchtime and evening. Just around the corner is The Wildfowler on the Wash, another village pub.

❹ Stay on the main track for about 0.75 mile (1.2km) beyond the farm, then go right by an old wartime pill box for a short path over to the sea wall.

❺ Turn right and follow either the grassy top of the sea bank (a public right of way) or the surfaced lane just below it past a succession of military observation towers. The bombing range is spread out before you, with the low Norfolk coast over to your right and the Lincolnshire seaboard towards Boston and Skegness leftwards.

❻ After the third tower ignore the gated road that heads off

### WHAT TO LOOK FOR

In an environment so featureless, the eye is inevitably drawn to a tiny, circular island, about a mile (1.6km) offshore near the mouth of the River Nene. It was built in 1975 as part of a study into the construction of freshwater reservoirs, but proved to be so popular with seabirds that the Fenland Wildfowlers' Association made it a permanent nesting site in 1987.

inland (a short cut back to Gedney), but instead continue along the sea bank past one final watchtower until you reach a stile. Cross the stile and continue for another 400yds (366m).

❼ Turn right at a public footpath sign, down some steps, for a direct path along a field-edge to the junction of an open lane. Here continue straight ahead into Gedney, turning right at the end back on to Dawsmere Road. However, if you want to prolong your Wash-side wander continue beyond the stile for 1.25 miles (2km) until the sea bank divides. Bend right, on the inland arm, and join a small lane before turning right on to Marsh Road back into Gedney Drove End.

### WHILE YOU'RE THERE

The River Nene enters the Wash near the small town of Sutton Bridge, 6 miles (9.7km) south of Gedney Drove End. Its historic swing bridge, built in 1897 by the Midland and Great Northern Railway Company, is one of the last surviving of its kind in the country, and connects Lincolnshire with Norfolk.

# The Banks of the Nene

*Enjoy a riverside meander around the
Northamptonshire town of Oundle.*

WALK 37

---

DISTANCE 6.75 miles (10.9km)   MINIMUM TIME 3hrs

ASCENT/GRADIENT 115ft (35m) ▲▲▲   LEVEL OF DIFFICULTY ✦✦✦

PATHS Waterside meadows and farmland tracks, 4 stiles

LANDSCAPE Winding river valley with woods and open pasture

SUGGESTED MAP OS Explorer 227 Peterborough

START/FINISH Grid reference: TL 042881

DOG FRIENDLINESS On lead through fields of livestock

PARKING Oundle town centre (long-stay car park off East Road)

PUBLIC TOILETS By short-stay car park off St Osyths Lane

---

The popular paths along this stretch of the Nene form part of 'Oundle Riverside Walks', a series of routes that are usefully waymarked and described on a leaflet available from the tourist information centre on West Street, Oundle. Some of it is also the route of the Nene Way, a long distance recreational trail of 110 miles (177km) that follows the course of the river from one of its three sources near Badby in Northamptonshire across Cambridgeshire to its mouth at Sutton Bridge in Lincolnshire, where it exits into the Wash (see Walk 36).

During its early, meandering progress through Northamptonshire the Nene is rich in deposits of sand and gravel, and their extraction has left a long series of pits and lakes around Northampton, Wellingborough and Thrapston that are now used for recreation and conservation. One collection just to the south of Oundle, has been transformed into Barnwell Country Park, an outdoor area with a visitor centre and wildlife garden.

## Keen on the Nene

The Nene is navigable from Northampton, where its three tributaries combine and an arm of the Grand Union Canal joins the river at Cotton End Lock. It forms an important part of Britain's inland waterways system, linking the Grand Union Canal to the River Great Ouse via what's known as the Middle Level System. Beyond Peterborough the Nene crosses the Fens and becomes a different river, often canalised and carefully regulated, and tidal over the last 26 miles (42km) below Dog in a Doublet Lock.

## Built in Stone

Oundle is famous for its public school, which is housed in a series of impressive buildings around the town. The original Laxton Grammar School was boys-only, but today Oundle School is co-educational. Most of the buildings in the centre of Oundle, fortunately preserved by a conservation order, are built from local limestone with Collyweston slate roofs (a gentle blue-green tile). They span several centuries, and include the Talbot Hotel, said to incorporate a stone staircase taken from the ruins

# OUNDLE

of Fotheringhay Castle, and St Peter's Church, whose 208ft (63m) spire is visible from the riverside path. Oundle Museum, in the old courthouse on Mill Road and open weekend afternoons (March to November), explores the town's development over the last 2,000 years, and includes a number of Roman and Saxon finds.

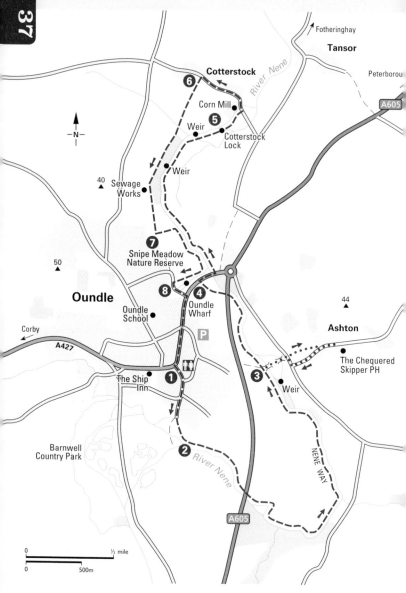

## WALK 37 DIRECTIONS

❶ From the end of Market Place, in the centre of Oundle, walk down St Osyths Lane, then South

Road until it curves right, then go straight on into Bassett Ford Road. Where this bends left into Riverside Close go ahead to the gate at the end. There are two

# OUNDLE

riverside walks indicated – make sure to go half left across the field and follow the bank downstream (not over the footbridge ahead).

**2** For the next 2.25 miles (3.6km) the route follows the bank of the Nene as it completes a giant loop. Go underneath Oundle bypass and eventually out by open meadows.

**3** Eventually, beyond a weir, you reach a long, high footbridge where you have the chance to cross the river for a visit to the picturesque village of Ashton (see Where to Eat and Drink), a round trip of 0.75 mile (1.2km). Otherwise continue straight ahead and back under the bypass to reach the old bridge.

**4** Cross over the road and turn right across the bridge. On the far side of the river turn left at the Riverside Walk sign, past the boat sheds, and strike out along the flat eastern bank of the Nene via two weirs. Take the path around the second weir and cross the footbridge to continue walking along the riverside path.

**5** Cross the river via the so-called 'guillotine' lock and continue to the lane at the far end

by a converted corn mill. Turn left and walk through the pretty village of Cotterstock, and after 550yds (503m) turn left before a red telephone box for a narrow path between a fence and hedge.

**6** This heads out along the left-hand side of an open field, then beside a narrow plantation with the river on the far side. Continue past a sewage works and directly down through two more fields before reaching a playing field.

**7** Half-way along the pitch turn left for a gap in the hedge and a boardwalk out to the Nene – this is a permissive route through Snipe Meadow nature reserve. Turn right and walk along the river bank until just before the bridge, then head right for Oundle Wharf. Go through a field beside the buildings to reach New Road.

**8** Turn left to the end of the road, then right into Station Road/ North Street to the town centre.

MANEA

# Fenland's Big Skies

*An enigmatic landscape links remote Manea with an historic drainage cut.*

DISTANCE 6.25 miles (10.1km) **MINIMUM TIME** 3hrs

ASCENT/GRADIENT Negligible ▲▲▲ **LEVEL OF DIFFICULTY** ✦✦✦

PATHS Lanes and hard farm tracks, field-edge paths, 1 stile

LANDSCAPE Wide, flat fields separated by ditches and drainage channels

SUGGESTED MAP OS Explorer 228 March & Ely

START/FINISH Grid reference: TL 478893

DOG FRIENDLINESS On lead at Ouse Washes Nature Reserve

PARKING Roadside parking in centre of Manea

PUBLIC TOILETS Off Park Road, Manea, and at Ouse Washes Nature Reserve

A landscape that is as flat and bare as the Fens may seem a dull and uninteresting prospect for a walk, but in fact there is much more to this unique place than first meets the eye, and what you see now isn't the way it looked in the distant past. Ancient tree trunks known as bog oaks are periodically uncovered from the peaty soil, proving that this apparently tree-less country once presented a totally different scene.

Until 400 years ago the Fens remained an unwelcoming swampy and impenetrable landscape which local outlaws and tribesmen such as Hereward the Wake, who led his rebels against the invading Normans, could make their own. Small communities such as Manea developed on the pockets of higher ground – the 'ea' suffix is derived from the Anglo-Saxon 'ig' meaning island.

## Draining the Fens

Systematic draining did not begin until the 17th century, when the 4th Earl of Bedford turned to Dutch engineer Cornelius Vermuyden to repeat his successful work in the Netherlands. The result was a direct, 20-mile (32km) cut known as the Old Bedford River, which sliced through the lands south and east of Manea taking the winter floodwaters out to the Wash. A rapidly expanding series of drains and dykes followed, gradually turning the ancient bog and swamp into fertile agricultural land, with many of these artificial rivers named after their original width (the New Bedford River is also known as the Hundred Foot Drain, for instance).

But not everyone agreed with the draining of the Fens, however, and there was determined opposition from the 'Fen Tigers', those wildfowlers and marshmen whose livelihoods depended on the traditional Fenland way of life. Even after the drains and dykes became permanent fixtures there were still, until quite recently, occasional throwbacks to another era. When transport and communication proved difficult, particularly for remote communities during the winter floods, the so-called Floating Church would go from hamlet to village providing religious services. The converted barge was still in use into the early years of the 20th century, when it spent two years tied up at Welches Dam, near Manea, which you visit on this walk.

# MANEA

## Fenland's Capital that Never Was

An early supporter of the ambitious drainage scheme was King Charles I, who owned 12,000 acres (4,860ha) of wetland surrounding Manea. He backed the enterprise of the early speculators to such an extent that he even took the lead in designing a brand new capital for the Fens. Complete with a royal palace for himself, the town was to be sited near Manea and would be called Charlemont. Alas, he unfortunately lost his head before his dream could be realised.

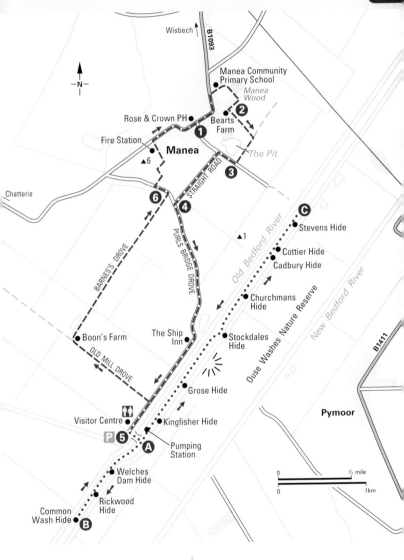

## WALK 38 DIRECTIONS

❶ With the Rose & Crown pub on your left, walk eastwards along Manea High Street and follow it round to the left as it becomes Station Road, then turn right for the public footpath alongside the primary school. At the football pitch at the far end turn right and go past Manea Wood, planted in 1997 for the local community with ash, oak, white willow, birch and common alder. Continue along the path as it bears right and approaches Bearts Farm.

## WHERE TO EAT AND DRINK

The Rose and Crown pub on Manea's High Street has limited opening hours, as does the nearby fish and chip shop on Station Road. The Ship Inn at Purls Bridge makes a good mid-way lunch stop, or you can take a picnic to the Ouse Washes Nature Reserve from the supermarket in Park Road at the start of the walk.

❷ Turn left by the old barns and sheds for the wide track out into the fields, and bear right at a junction of tracks to reach an attractive reedy lake known locally as 'the Pit'. This was originally dug for clay, which was then transported across the fields on a light railway to shore up the banks of the nearby Old and New Bedford Rivers. The Pit is now a popular place for fishermen and wildlife alike.

❸ At the end of the track turn right on to a lane, with the lake still on your right, then, when you reach the junction at the corner of the road, turn left, on to Straight Road, and follow this through the fields to the end.

❹ Turn left on to Purls Bridge Drove, signposted 'Welches Dam' and 'RSPB reserve'. Follow this open lane all the way to Purls Bridge, by the Old Bedford River. Continue along the bank to reach the Ouse Washes Nature Reserve, where there's a visitor centre and public toilets.

❺ Return along the lane for 440yds (402m) and turn left for

## WHAT TO LOOK FOR

The area around Manea is sometimes known as the Black Fens, because of its dark-coloured soils which are chiefly derived from peat. The high-yielding land means that intensive arable farming dominates, with very little livestock. As you walk through the vast, hedgeless fields look about you – depending on the time of year you may see huge fields of onions, potatoes, cereals, sugar beet, carrots or oilseed rape.

the signposted public bridleway by some dark wooden sheds. Known as Old Mill Drove, this runs directly across the open fields as far as the rusting farm machinery and outbuildings of Boon's Farm. Turn right and walk along the dead-straight Barnes's Drove for 1.25 miles (2km) until you reach the road at the far end.

## WHILE YOU'RE THERE

The Wisbech and Fenland Museum in the centre of Wisbech has a fascinating display exploring the landscape and history of the Fens. The museum, housed in a purpose-built Victorian building with many of its period fixtures and fittings, has other wide-ranging displays and exhibits that include the original manuscript of Charles Dickens's *Great Expectations* and an ivory chess set that once belonged to Louis XIV.

❻ Turn left and after 150yds (137m) turn off right through a gate for a public footpath across the fields back into Manea. The route zig-zags between a series of paddocks – just follow the clear yellow waymarks and aim for the fire station tower. At the far side cross a stile and turn right, past the village stores, to follow the main road back to the centre.

# Twitching in Ouse Washes

*A short hide-by-hide wander along the Ouse Washes Nature Reserve.*
**See map and information panel for Walk 38**

---

DISTANCE *up to 10 miles (16.1km) depending on hides visited*

MINIMUM TIME *up to 5hrs*

ASCENT/GRADIENT *Negligible* ▲▲▲   LEVEL OF DIFFICULTY ✦✦✦

---

## WALK 39 DIRECTIONS (Walk 38 option)

The Ouse Washes Nature Reserve is run by the Royal Society for the Protection of Birds (RSPB) and Cambridgeshire Wildlife Trust. Entrance is free throughout the year. The reserve covers 2,471 acres (1,000ha) of wet grassland that lie in a wide strip almost 20 miles (32 km) long and 1 mile (1.6km) wide between the Old and New Bedford Rivers. These two artificial cuts are backed by huge embankments that were designed to act as a storage tank when the winter rains would otherwise have flooded the land.

Today the area forms the largest area of regularly flooding 'washland' in Britain, and after the flood waters have subsided ducks and waders nest in the fields before cattle are introduced in the summer to keep the grass and sedge short.

In winter, ducks, such as pochard, garganey, teal and pintail, are all regular visitors, plus the likes of migrating Bewick's and whooper swans. Over 53,000 wigeon dropped by during the winter of 1989–9.

Summer has its own attractions, including lapwings and kingfishers, and perhaps the sight of a marsh harrier gliding low over the ground in search of his tea. The network of dykes and pools also supports other wildlife such as dragonflies.

Access to the nature reserve is limited to the bank of the Old Bedford Barrier, which defines its western edge.

The ten hides are all free to enter, and binoculars are even available to borrow at the visitor centre near Welches Dam (open daily, 9am to 5pm). From here cross the bridge by the pumping station (Point **Ⓐ**) and turn right for the hides known as Welches Dam, Rickwood and Common Wash (Point **Ⓑ**), the furthest of which is just under 1 mile (1.6km) distant.

For the more remote and undisturbed hides turn left by the pump house and walk along the bottom of the bank rather than the top (so as not to scare the birds). The furthest is Stevens Hide (Point **Ⓒ**), just under 2 miles (3.2km) away. In each hide there are identification charts and wide views across this arresting landscape towards the outline of Ely Cathedral.

# The Glory of Ely Cathedral

*Explore Cambridgeshire's lovely
cathedral city of Ely on this short trail.*

| | |
|---|---|
| **DISTANCE** 3.25 miles (5.3km) | **MINIMUM TIME** 1hr 30min |
| **ASCENT/GRADIENT** 100ft (30m) ▲▲▲ | **LEVEL OF DIFFICULTY** +++ |

**PATHS** Surfaced tracks and pavements, field and woodland paths

**LANDSCAPE** Fenland city, magnificent cathedral, busy waterfront

**SUGGESTED MAP** OS Explorer 226 Ely & Newmarket

**START/FINISH** Grid reference: TL 538800

**DOG FRIENDLINESS** Poop scoop bins are provided around city

**PARKING** Barton Road car park (free)

**PUBLIC TOILETS** By cathedral, Market Place, Quayside and car park

## WALK 40 DIRECTIONS

If it wasn't for the cathedral, Ely would properly be called a town, because its layout makes it just the right size to be explored on foot. But don't be fooled by the short distance of this walk – there is so much to see that you could easily spend a whole day wandering among the historic buildings and still manage to miss out on the home-made cakes in the cathedral's Refectory Café.

From the Barton Road car park, walk towards the cathedral and turn left on to Silver Street, then right on to St Mary's Street to reach the tourist information centre. This is a good place to start, not least because the 13th-century building was Oliver Cromwell's former home and houses a small exhibition. Walk past St Mary's parish church to reach Palace Green and the glorious west face of Ely Cathedral.

St Etheldreda, Queen of Northumbria, first established a monastery here in AD 673, and 400 years later the Normans began work on the mighty building you see today. It's affectionately known as the Ship of the Fens, partly because Ely was sited on a small island that rose out of the swampy Fenland so that the hilltop cathedral, with its huge octagonal tower rising up like a colossal mast, dominates the view for miles around.

Walk along the left-hand side of the cathedral on Steeple Row and follow the semi-circular path all the way around to the far side (the gates close at 6:30pm). Go down the street opposite, past various monastic buildings including the Priory and Canonry Houses, as far

### WHAT TO LOOK FOR

Inside Ely Cathedral is the Stained Glass Museum (open daily), dedicated to the rescue and display of stained glass. The main exhibition has over 100 separate panels tracing the ancient craft from the Middle Ages to the present day. There are group tours and workshops for those curious about stained glass.

as the Porta Gate. This imposing 14th-century gateway to Ely monastery is now the library of The King's School, East Anglia's oldest independent school. Don't go through the gateway, but turn around to follow a surfaced path by a fence down through Ely Park. To your left, across the Meadow, there are new and stunning views of the cathedral, framed by trees, while the mound in the trees to your right represents the remains of a motte-and-bailey castle.

At the bottom of the hill leave the park and cross Broad Street, then continue down to the River Great Ouse via the new Jubilee Gardens, opened by the Duke of Edinburgh in 2002 as part of Ely's Golden Jubilee celebrations. Turn left and walk along the busy waterfront, past the old Maltings as far as the bridge to the marina. If you want to shorten the route and avoid the field and woodland paths veer left here for a pavement walk up Fore Hill back to Market Place near the cathedral.

Otherwise continue along Pegasus Walk, waterside of the Babylon Gallery. Beyond an open strip of

willows continue underneath the railway bridge and out across an open meadow. Once upon a time the River Great Ouse provided a useful catch for the local inhabitants. Ely's name comes from 'Eelig', meaning eel island, and for a while local taxes were even payable in eels.

With the railway on your left, keep on the main path that drifts away from the river bank across the middle of the field. Go through a gate at the far side and turn left on to a narrow path. At the end turn left and walk along Kiln Lane, over a level crossing, and go immediately left on to a wide path through trees (signposted 'Hereward Way'). Across to the right are the flooded Roswell Pits, dug for clay and now managed for wildlife.

Follow this straight and obvious track known as Springhead Lane through the light woodland for over 0.25 mile (400m), ignoring paths off either side. At the far end it emerges to bend right and cross a road. Go up a wide grassy strip between houses and after 100yds (91m) turn left, indicated 'public footpath', for a passageway between buildings. At the end go right, then immediately left, at the bottom of Vineyard Way. Walk along this street (aiming for the cathedral, now in sight) to emerge at Market Place.

Walk up the pedestrianised Market Street to the very end where Ely Museum (closed Tuesday) is housed in the former Bishops' Gaol and still retains the original hidden doorways, wall-planking and prisoners' graffiti. Turn left into Lynn Street. Walk past The Lamb hotel and straight ahead at the road junction to return to the cathedral and Palace Green.

# A Village Trail from Badby

*This route links three delightful
villages west of Northampton.*

---

**DISTANCE** 6.75 miles (10.9km)   **MINIMUM TIME** 3hrs 30min

**ASCENT/GRADIENT** 787ft (240m) ▲▲▲   **LEVEL OF DIFFICULTY** +++

**PATHS** Mostly pasture, muddy where cows congregate, 11 stiles

**LANDSCAPE** Undulating hills covered with fields, woods and parkland

**SUGGESTED MAP** OS Explorer 207 Newport Pagnell & Northampton South

**START/FINISH** Grid reference: SP 559589

**DOG FRIENDLINESS** Plenty of livestock, so strict control necessary, lots of stiles

**PARKING** On Main Street, Badby

**PUBLIC TOILETS** None on route (nearest in Daventry)

---

Between Badby and Fawsley you will be following the Knightley Way, a handily waymarked trail that stretches 12 miles (19.4km) from Badby to Greens Norton, near Towcester, and is named after the family that lived at Fawsley Hall for 500 years.

The Knightleys moved to Fawsley from Staffordshire in the 1600s and, although considerably refashioned several hundred years later, the original vaulted Great Hall of their Tudor mansion is retained in what is now a country hotel, complete with Georgian and Victorian wings. It also boasts the Queen Elizabeth I Chamber, named after the Monarch who apparently stayed in the very room while on a visit in 1575.

In addition to the new house the Knightleys also 'imparked' the village, which meant that they created their own private parkland, turning local arable land into pasture for their animals and in the process evicting most of the village. This explains why only the 14th-century Church of St Mary the Virgin is left, standing isolated before the hall. It contains the tomb of Sir Richard Fawsley, knighted by Henry VIII.

## From Village to Park

The English Midlands have a particularly high proportion of deserted villages and, as the county of 'spires and squires', Northamptonshire's gentry was quite adept at turfing out the commoners without a moment's notice. Time and again the villagers were squeezed out so his lordship could graze his flocks of sheep or herds of cattle, or fatten up his all-important deer without interference. Enclosure was at its height in the late 15th and early 16th centuries, and not helped by depopulation through plagues.

Two hundred years later, when the fashion for grand landscaped parks was reaching its height, buildings and sometimes even whole communities were moved so that the view from the main house or hall across the parkland could be 'improved' and uninterrupted. For instance, the old village of Wimpole (see Walk 50) was moved to a new site outside the park.

The term 'park' originally meant simply a piece of ground used for hunting, and enclosure through imparking ultimately led to the creation of the numerous stately parks that you see scattered across the Midlands today. Other notable Northamptonshire estates include the Marquess of Northampton's Castle Ashby (see Walk 42) and Althorp, seat of the Spencer family, while across the Bedfordshire border is the Duke of Bedford's 3,000-acre (1,215ha) Woburn Abbey.

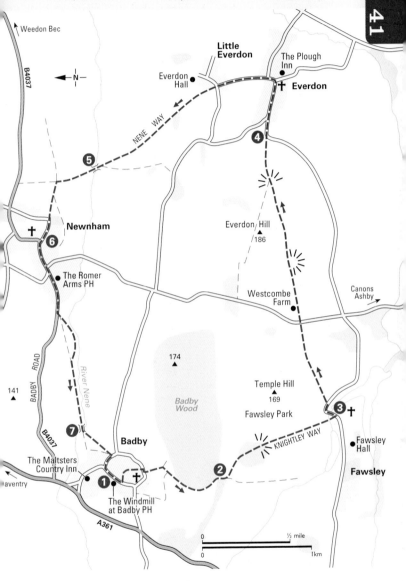

## WALK 41 DIRECTIONS

❶ With your back to The Windmill at Badby, walk up Vicarage Hill to reach Badby church. Take the alleyway path signposted 'Fawsley', opposite the south side of the church, then head right up a sloping field for a path around the western edge of Badby Wood, famous for its springtime bluebells.

❷ After about 0.25 mile (400m) take the right fork (upper path), and follow waymarks for the Knightley Way out across the open hilltop of Fawsley Park and down towards the lakes near the hall.

❸ Go ahead along the lane at the bottom to inspect the church, otherwise turn left, and in a few paces left again (before the cattle grid) for a footpath that heads up and across a large sloping field. Go through a gate and down a track to the road, then resume opposite climbing steadily through fields, passing Westcombe Farm on the left. Continue across Everdon Hill and down to the village of Everdon below, joining a lane via a stile to the right as you near the bottom of the hill.

❹ Walk through the village, following the road as it bends left past the church and pub, and turn left for the lane to reach Little Everdon. When the road appears to split go ahead/left for a path to the left of the farm buildings. This continues out across open fields, with Everdon Hall to your right. On the far side, pass the end of a strip of trees and maintain your north-westerly direction to carry on through four more fields and reach the river (aim just to the right of Newnham's church spire when it comes into view).

❺ Cross the Nene via a footbridge and walk uphill through one field, then veer left in the second to cross a third, and drop down to pick up a farm drive which, beyond a gate, becomes Manor Lane. Walk on to join the main street.

❻ Turn left and drop down past the pub by The Green and continue along Badby Road out of the village. In 150yds (137m) go left for field-edge paths alongside the infant River Nene.

❼ Go over the footbridge at the end and walk half left through the field ahead, keeping left of the clump of trees in the middle and aiming for Badby church. At the far corner turn right into Chapel Lane to return to the centre of Badby.

CASTLE ASHBY

# A Fine State
# of Affairs

*A varied walk that takes in a leisurely
river and a grandiose mansion.*

---

DISTANCE 6.5 miles (10.4km)  MINIMUM TIME 3hrs

ASCENT/GRADIENT 557ft (170m) ▲▲▲  LEVEL OF DIFFICULTY ✦✦✦

PATHS Field paths, farm tracks and river bank, some steps

LANDSCAPE Low rolling hills above gentle Nene Valley

SUGGESTED MAP OS Explorer 207 Newport Pagnell &
Northampton South

START/FINISH Grid reference: SP 859594

DOG FRIENDLINESS Mostly arable fields, so generally good

PARKING Roadside in Castle Ashby, or car park for visitors

PUBLIC TOILETS Rural Shopping Yard, Castle Ashby

---

Castle Ashby is the ancestral home of the 7th Marquess of Northampton,
and a fine pile he has too. Building work began in 1574 under the
direction of the 1st Lord Compton, later Earl of Northampton, who
originally had the house built in the shape of an 'E' before the architect
Inigo Jones filled in the openings. Altogether the estate covers 10,000 acres
(4,050ha) and is surrounded by landscaped parkland designed by Lancelot
('Capability') Brown. But aside from the neat lake and vast manicured
lawns, the eye-catching feature has to be the stunning, mile-long avenue,
first planted in 1695 after a visit by William III.

Castle Ashby House is closed to the public, but the 200-acre (81ha)
gardens are open daily – to get there, follow the signs through the village
and across the avenue in front of the house. They include an arboretum and
conservatory, and a more formal Victorian terrace and romantic Italianate
designs. The latter reflected the 19th-century revival of interest in classical
Italian gardens, which were based on the use of steps and balustrades, and
on a structured transition that began with a geometrical layout through to
more serpentine and irregular shapes. Parterres (formal floral beds) were
created, using the family's crest as a motif.

Today there are many different varieties of trees and shrubs, including
a giant horse chestnut described as one of the largest spreading trees in
Britain, plus landscaped lawns and lakes complete with ornamental bridges
and the so-called Triumphal Arch. And if you want to take some of it
home with you there's an area of plant sales, including shrubs, herbaceous
perennials and alpines all nurtured on the premises. Next to the gardens
you can visit the 14th-century Church of St Mary Magdalene, which has
various monuments to the Compton family.

## Rural Shopping Yard

The estate also manages the craft yard in the centre of the village (it's also
referred to as the rather more down-to-earth 'Rural Shopping Yard'). Open
Tuesday to Sunday, here you will find a wide range of ceramics and pottery,

antiques and world crafts, bespoke furniture and a quality delicatessen, plus inviting tea rooms serving cakes and other refreshments.

## Close to the Knuckle

The perimeter of the vast Castle Ashby estate is dotted, as you would imagine, with various lodges and gatehouses. But there's one that's rather different to the rest. Knucklebone Lodge (which sadly is private and cannot be visited) is so-called because of its knucklebone-patterned floor. But the thing is they are real animals' knucklebones, apparently belonging to what amounted to several thousand sheep, and which were painstakingly arranged into a complete floor covering. Recycling it may be, but it really makes you want to reach for the carpet catalogue, doesn't it.

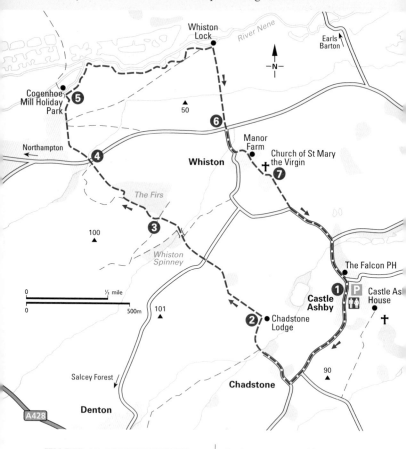

## WALK 42 DIRECTIONS

**1** Walk out of Castle Ashby along the road heading south westwards, with the house (and visitors' car park) over to your left. Where the pavement ends turn right for Chadstone. Drop down the lane past the cottages and expensive-looking converted barns and all the way out of the hamlet to the farm of Chadstone Lodge.

**2** Turn left for the bridleway behind the hedge and, at the end, go on through the trees to continue the route alongside the next field and down to a road.

Cross over for a footpath down to Whiston Spinney, then via a footbridge in a lovely shady dell to reach a junction of tracks on the far side. Here go straight on, and climb directly up the sloping field ahead to the trees on the far side.

❸ Follow the path into the woods to climb some steps and head out along a field-edge with woodland on your right. Beyond a gate go down a sharp flight of steps to the right and across a field in order to turn left on the far side and drop down to the road below.

❹ The route continues up through the field opposite. Head half left, then follow the bridleway waymarks to the right, through a long narrow field with the houses of Cogenhoe on your left. At the far side join a lane and descend to Cogenhoe Mill.

❺ Just before the old mill buildings and sluice, with the holiday park beyond, turn right for a path alongside the River Nene (signposted 'Nene Way'). Follow this pleasant waterside walk for 1 mile (1.6km) as far as Whiston Lock, then turn right for a straight farm track across the fields to the main road, heading towards Whiston church sitting astride the hilltop like a lighthouse.

❻ Go across the junction and walk along the lane into Whiston,

branching left at the small triangular village green. Take the gated passageway beside the outbuildings of Manor Farm up to the church. There are good views across the Nene Valley to Earls Barton and Wellingborough, and the eastern edge of Northampton.

## WHILE YOU'RE THERE

A few miles to the south-west of Castle Ashby is Salcey Forest, which was once part of a large medieval hunting chase. Today it's managed by the Forestry Commission and makes a good day out for people of all ages. There are walking and cycle trails, a children's playground and café, and a Tree Top Way offering bird's-eye views over the forest.

❼ Walk past the church to the far side of the churchyard, go over a metal rung in the wall and turn right on to an obvious field-edge path. This continues along a grassy strip between further fields and emerges on to the bend of a lane. Go straight on/left to walk this all the way back to Castle Ashby.

## WHAT TO LOOK FOR

St Mary's Church above Whiston is a prominent local landmark, its striking tower resplendent in alternating bands of yellow and grey limestone. Unaltered since it was completed in 1534, it can only be reached on foot, and repays an unhurried and contemplative visit.

## WHERE TO EAT AND DRINK

The Buttery is housed in the craft yard and serves hot and cold snacks and meals from mid-morning to mid-afternoon. There are also a few outside seats in the yard, and it's a good place to start and finish the day's walk. Near by is The Falcon, an upmarket pub serving bar snacks and full meals. The Walled Garden Tea Room in the gardens of Castle Ashby house is open daily in summer and winter weekends.

# Flying Kites
# in Rockingham

*Discover a remnant of Northamptonshire's ancient forest,*
*which is now home to red kites — magnificent birds of prey.*

W A L K

4 3

---

**DISTANCE** 5 miles (8km)   **MINIMUM TIME** 2hrs 30min

**ASCENT/GRADIENT** 426ft (130m) ▲▲▲   **LEVEL OF DIFFICULTY** ✦✦✦

**PATHS** Firm forest tracks, woodland and field paths, 8 stiles

**LANDSCAPE** Mixed woodland, surrounded by undulating farmland

**SUGGESTED MAP** OS Explorers 224 Corby, Kettering & Wellingborough or 234 Rutland Water

**START/FINISH** Grid reference: SP 979982

**DOG FRIENDLINESS** Generally very good, but on lead visiting wildlife site

**PARKING** Forestry Commission car park, Fineshade Wood (off A43)

**PUBLIC TOILETS** At visitor centre

---

The term 'forest' originally meant a loose collection of neighbouring but separate woods, and Rockingham Forest, which once spread from Peterborough to Oxford, still bears that out. However, the few remaining pockets of this ancient forest are now considerably shrunken and isolated in Northamptonshire. Fineshade, Westhay, Wakerley and Fermyn woods are today managed by the Forestry Commission, and the emphasis is very squarely on conservation and responsible recreation. Partly because of that, Rockingham Forest has become one of the key centres for the reintroduction to the Midlands of one of our most majestic birds of prey.

The red kite is a magnificently handsome and truly impressive bird, huge in size (with a wing span of up to 5ft/1.5m), but incredibly agile. Several centuries ago they were a common sight across the country, even scavenging for left-overs in the centre of London. But long-term persecution led to their eventual extinction in England, and only as recently as the 1990s have they been carefully reintroduced to parts of the Chilterns, Yorkshire and the East Midlands, much to the delight of birders and wildlife enthusiasts.

The 'Red kites at Rockingham' display at the Forestry Commission's Top Lodge barn at Fineshade, organised in association with the RSPB, tells you much more about these magnificent birds. The RSPB shop features a CCTV link with a nest in the nearby forest so that you can watch them close-up (depending on whether and where the birds choose to nest, of course!) and there are also guided walks and talks throughout the year.

### Tresham's Follies

In addition to its numerous country houses and parks, Northamptonshire also has some splendid follies. In that department the county's chief architect was Sir Thomas Tresham, Elizabethan landowner and persecuted Catholic who designed a number of odd buildings that still can't quite be figured out today. Rushton Triangular Lodge, north west of Kettering, is made up of three 33-ft (10m) sides, three storeys, three gables on each side, and so on, while Lyveden New Bield, south west of Oundle, is an

# ROCKINGHAM FOREST

apparently unfinished building in the shape of a Greek cross sitting isolated amid the fields. Experts have puzzled over Tresham's works for centuries, but are no nearer understanding what on earth they mean. A leaflet entitled the Tresham Trail is available from local tourist information centres.

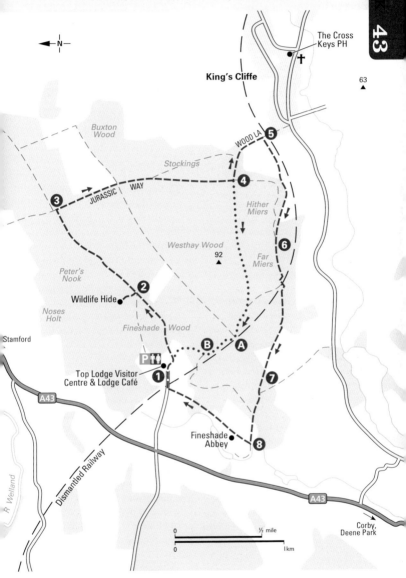

## WALK 43 DIRECTIONS

❶ With the Top Lodge visitor centre and café on your left, walk along the lane past the Forestry Commission's offices, and fork left where the track divides. After passing some houses, it soon becomes a wide, semi-surfaced forest drive.

❷ Just before you reach two semi-detached cottages (Nos 2 and 4 Top Lodge), you can detour for a broad gravel track on the left that leads through the trees to a wildlife hide (free to enter) overlooking an artificial pond and an area of open ground. Continue along the main track through pleasantly open woodland until, just after a mile (1.6km) from the start, you turn right at a crossroads of paths, indicated 'Jurassic Way'.

**3** Walk down this wide track through the trees, with a field soon opening up to the left. When the field ends, go straight over a junction of paths into Westhay Wood and, in a few paces, join a main forest track to continue south through the woodland.

**4** At the junction at the very far end, where the main track turns abruptly right, go left and walk through a small timber yard to

reach Wood Lane. Walk down as far as the old railway bridge.

**5** To visit the charming village of King's Cliffe continue to the bottom of the lane, cross over and turn left – the pub and church are at the far end of West Street. Otherwise turn right before the railway cutting for a field-edge footpath. When you reach the border of Westhay Wood continue through the fields alongside the woodland, until in the very far corner the path disappears into the trees.

**6** Follow the well-waymarked route (there are even direction arrows attached to some of the trees), which at one point crosses the former railway by the remains of an old footbridge. After following an old fence you eventually emerge into fields. Walk around the right-hand edge, beside the trees, until a clear path cuts across the corner to the woodland on the far side.

**7** Continue along the path through the conifers, then turn right on to a wide farm track that drops down, via a gate, on to the open hillside above Fineshade Abbey (private).

**8** Turn right along a fenced path above the buildings and on across a tree-covered hillside. Go over a wide and dipping field, then turn right on to the lane at the far side to reach the car park at the top.

# An Illuminating Short Cut

*Take an evening stroll and you might enjoy some unexpected natural lighting.*

**See map and information panel for Walk 43**

DISTANCE 3.5 miles (5.7km)   MINIMUM TIME 1hr 30min
ASCENT/GRADIENT 180ft (55m) ▲▲▲   LEVEL OF DIFFICULTY +++

## WALK 44 DIRECTIONS (Walk 43 option)

At Point **4**, where the main walk bears left for Wood Lane and King's Cliffe, go right to continue along the broad and easy track. The woodland here supports a healthy wildlife population. Besides the red kites, residents and visitors include dormice, nightingales, and several types of bat, and a walk at dusk may be illuminated, quite literally, by glow-worms. Britain has two varieties of these long, winged beetles, and the females like nothing better than sitting on the ground on warm, summer evenings, glowing blue-green to attract the males.

Ignore all other paths off left and right, and keep going west. Occasional waymarks indicate that this is also the route of the Jurassic Way, an 88-mile (142km) trail between Stamford in Lincolnshire (see Walk 35) and Banbury in Oxfordshire. It's named after the band of Jurassic limestone that runs through the East Midlands, and its symbol is an ammonite fossil.

A sign marks the boundary between Fineshade and Westhay Woods (Point **A**), where another forest ride enters from the right. Keep going straight on, as the track now bends a little to run alongside an overgrown railway cutting (on the left). The line was built in 1879 to connect the Northampton–Peterborough line at Yarwell Junction with the Rugby–Stamford line at Seaton in Rutland.

After 0.25 mile (400m) bear right at a broad junction of tracks (Point **B**), indicated by a Jurassic Way marker. Follow this all the way back to the surfaced lane at the end to return to the car park and visitor centre.

Although the Forestry Commission's useful map (available free of charge from the visitor centre) depicts Fineshade Wood as covering the entire northern half of their holdings, strictly speaking Fineshade Wood is just a small individual wood to the north-east – just as the great Rockingham Forest (like Sherwood Forest, see Walks 13 and 14) barely exists any more. Both Fineshade and Westhay woods comprise a number of smaller spinneys and copses known by a variety of delightful names (Noses Holt, Peter's Nook, Stockings, The Gullet, Hither Miers and Far Miers), while to the north of King's Cliffe the Woodland Trust has established a Millennium Woodland.

# In the Paxton Pit Lane

*A gentle stroll in a riverside nature reserve near St Neots in Cambridgeshire.*

**DISTANCE** 3.5 miles (5.7km)  **MINIMUM TIME** 1hr 30min

**ASCENT/GRADIENT** Negligible ▲▲▲  **LEVEL OF DIFFICULTY** ✚✚✚

**PATHS** Mostly firm tracks, boards across marshy ground

**LANDSCAPE** Reclaimed lakes, meadows, woodland and reed beds

**SUGGESTED MAP** OS Explorer 225 Huntingdon & St Ives

**START/FINISH** Grid reference: TL 196629

**DOG FRIENDLINESS** Mostly on lead, out of water at all times, use dog bins

**PARKING** Paxton Pits Nature Reserve, Little Paxton (signs from B1041)

**PUBLIC TOILETS** At visitors' centre

## WALK 45 DIRECTIONS

Located on the banks of the River Great Ouse, 1.5 miles (2.4km) north of St Neots, Paxton Pits Nature Reserve consists of a series of shallow lakes and ponds originally dug for gravel and sand extraction and now flooded for the benefit of wildlife. The industry continues near by, and if you visit mid-week you will probably see lorries rumbling by filled with gravel for the building industry. And yet these same pits and pools that were first scooped out over a century ago, and whose gravel was used to make runways during the Second World War and build roads and houses in the following decades, are now unrecognisable as peaceful, open lakes where kingfishers, grebes and terns are a common, and ducks such as gadwall and wigeon overwinter in large numbers.

Part of the nature reserve has been designated a Site of Special Scientific Interest (SSSI), for apart from the wetland and marsh the pits are surrounded by hay meadows and mixed woodland that provide entirely different types of habitat. Nightingales, for instance, regularly sing from the woods alongside Haul Road in April and May – a visit at either dawn or dusk is the best time to hear the males' song. Several waymarked nature trails criss-cross the reserve, whose eastern border is defined by the river bank of the tree-lined Great Ouse. During the school holidays there are special activities for children based at the visitors' centre (see www.paxton-pits.org.uk). St Neots Bird and Wildlife Club also organise a programme of talks and field trips throughout the year. So far 220 species of birds have

### WHILE YOU'RE THERE

St Neots is Cambridgeshire's largest market town with a diverse range of facilities. The Riverside Park is a popular place for recreation. The museum in the former police station on New Street, near the Market Square, tells the story of the town over the centuries, and has workshops and changing exhibitions.

been recorded on the reserve, with around 70 breeding. Rarities include a black kite, little egret and honey buzzard.

Take the gated path behind the visitors' centre indicated 'Meadow Trail', and follow this lovely, wandering route past Rudd and Cloudy Lakes, small reed-lined pits filled with water lilies and bulrushes (also known as reed mace). This is a key area for insects during the summer months, including butterflies like the marbled white and purple hairstreak, and over 300 different types of moth. At the far end go up the steps and turn left on to a straight, tree-lined track, and soon Hayling Lake appears through the undergrowth on the right.

> ### WHERE TO EAT AND DRINK
>
> The Visitors' Centre is open at weekends for hot drinks and snacks; otherwise try The Anchor on Little Paxton High Street or The Village Bistro near the A1 junction.

At the junction at the far end turn left and follow the Riverside Trail for 0.75 mile (1.2km). The path sticks closely to the river bank with open farmland and meadows to the left. It then heads inland and turns away from the river and shortly afterwards you turn right by a notice board on to a gravel track just past (but not at) the signposted 'river viewpoint'.

This is also the route of the Ouse Valley Way, a 26-mile (42km) long-distance trail that follows the river over its Cambridgeshire flood plain. Eventually you leave its helpful waymarks behind and veer away from the river just past a wooden post (No 12) for the Heron circular nature trail. Go left, then right, on to a wide gravel track between the two lakes known as Heronry North and Washout Pit, where feeding geese are a common sight.

Signs warn against swimming in the deep, cold water, and also of the dangers of quicksand! The reason becomes a little clearer further on as you approach the still-active quarry, where oddly shaped machines (there's an information board that tells you what each does) dig away and grade the aggregate. The waymarked public footpath treads its way through the works, past the site office and weighbridge, and at the far side turns left on to a grassy path adjacent to the lane.

Before long the path merges with the tree-lined lane, known as Haul Road, and you should follow this wide thoroughfare all the way back to the car park. There are several optional diversions through the trees on the left that allow useful vantage points over the large lagoon known as Heronry South. When you arrive at the main junction before the visitors' centre turn left, through the gates, for a short detour to visit two bird hides. Apart from the activity on the water, scan the tree tops on the far side for a view of the nesting cormorants, which began with a single pair in 1988 and now number around 120.

> ### WHAT TO LOOK FOR
>
> On warm, sunny days between May and September look out for damselflies and dragonflies, especially along the banks of the River Great Ouse. Paxton Pits supports several varieties of each, including the common blue and blue-tailed damselflies, and the southern and brown hawker dragonflies, many of which have set routes and flying times.

*Overleaf: Heronry South Lake at Paxton Pits Nature Reserve (Walk 45)*

# Wicken – the Last Survivor

*Step back in time through an authentic Cambridgeshire fen, virtually the last of its kind left in Britain.*

WALK 46

---

DISTANCE 4.75 miles (7.7km)  MINIMUM TIME 2hrs

ASCENT/GRADIENT *Negligible* ▲▲▲  LEVEL OF DIFFICULTY +++

PATHS *Mostly river banks and farm tracks, potentially slippery*

LANDSCAPE *Low-lying fenland of dykes, scrub and open fields*

SUGGESTED MAP *OS Explorer 226 Ely & Newmarket*

START/FINISH *Grid reference: TL 564706*

DOG FRIENDLINESS *Under close control due to livestock and nesting wildlife*

PARKING *Wicken Fen nature reserve car park (pay-and-display) if visiting the reserve, otherwise off Wicken High Street*

PUBLIC TOILETS *At nature reserve car park and visitor centre*

---

Wicken Fen is one of the oldest nature reserves in the country and, as the last surviving remnant of original fenland left in Britain, one of the most important, too. Over the last 400 years over 99 per cent of East Anglia's ancient Great Fen has been drained and converted into farmland, richly productive for agriculture, but largely sterile for wildlife.

Not surprisingly the National Trust's 1,600 acres (648ha) at Wicken have assumed a critical importance. Since they purchased their first tiny piece of land here in 1899, the Trust has made over 60 separate acquisitions at Wicken, and the plan is to continue to add to their holdings by acquiring farmland to the south of the reserve and restoring it to its original wetland state. The ultimate aim is to create a nature reserve covering 10,000 acres (4,050ha) between Cambridge and Wicken Fen.

## Wildlife at Wicken

The nature reserve itself includes a short boardwalk (0.75 miles/1.2km) and a longer nature trail (2.25 miles/3.6km), while eight hides allow close-up views over the many ponds and ditches which, depending on the time of year, are often teeming with wildlife. For instance, Wicken Fen hosts more than 1,000 types of beetle, and visiting coleopterists (that's beetle-lovers to you and me) once included the young Charles Darwin who came here to collect specimens while studying at Cambridge.

As well as 212 species of spider, Wicken Fen also supports nearly 300 different types of plant. In the summer the ponds and pools buzz with dragonflies and damselflies, and are full of yellow and white water lilies, water mint and water violets, plus the greater bladderwort, a carnivorous plant with small yellow flowers and virtually no roots that feasts on small aquatic life forms. Away from the water the uncultivated grassland features early marsh and southern marsh orchids, usually flowering in June, while in the areas of sedge you can find milk parsley and the light purple flowers of the rare marsh pea. A visit to the reserve is a must, and you should allow the bare minimum of an hour to explore.

# WICKEN FEN

## Managing the Land

An on-going programme of management is essential to maintain the distinctive character of the land. For generations Wicken peat has been cut for burning, and sedge (a grass-like plant that grows on wet ground) has been harvested for thatching. The peat is now untouched, but sedge is still cut every three years in the summer – just as it has been at Wicken ever since 1419. Meanwhile konig ponies, already used in the Norfolk Broads, have been introduced to Verrall's Fen to stop cleared scrub from reinvading; and ditches are periodically dredged of choking vegetation by a process with the splendid name of 'slubbing'.

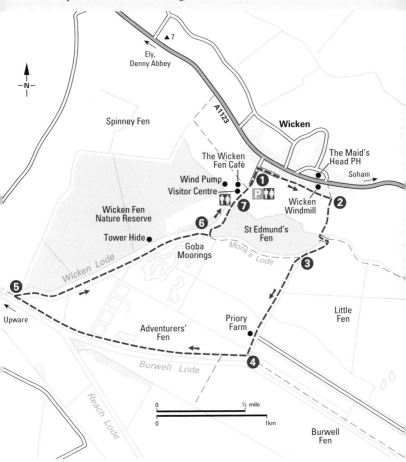

## WALK 46 DIRECTIONS

❶ From the nature reserve car park walk up Lode Lane towards the village of Wicken. Before you meet the main road turn right on to Back Lane and follow this route, which soon becomes a pleasant track running behind the houses. When you reach the far end of the lane, just after a windmill, turn right on to a wide track through the fields. (If you have parked in the centre of the village take the signposted public footpath via Cross Green, just along from and opposite the pub, out to the fields.)

**2** Follow this wide route down to two footbridges. Cross the second bridge and turn right along the bank of Monk's Lode, with St Edmund's Fen opposite. A lode, incidentally, is another name for an artificially cut waterway.

**3** After 550yds (503m) branch left before a fence and gate for a long straight track, known as a drove, and head out across the fields to Priory Farm. Join the surfaced lane and continue all the way to the end.

**4** Turn right by the raised Cockup Bridge and walk along the bank of the Burwell Lode (don't be tempted by the footbridge). Continue for 1.5 miles (2.4km) past Adventurers' Fen, named after the 17th-century 'Gentlemen Adventurers' who first started draining the fens in earnest.

**5** At a high-arched footbridge over Wicken Lode turn right and walk along this bank back towards Wicken Fen past a National Trust sign. If you continue across the footbridge and walk for another 0.25 mile (400m) you come to Upware, with a pub (see Where to Eat and Drink) and picnic area. Ignoring paths off into the open fen and fields on your right,

continue along the bank until its junction with Monk's Lode. Across the water you pass the lofty thatched Tower Hide.

**6** Cross the short bridge by Goba Moorings and continue alongside Wicken Lode, not along Monk's Lode (to the right). The lush vegetation of Wicken Fen is now either side.

**7** When you get to the end turn left to the visitor centre (open daily from Easter to October, Tuesday to Sunday in winter). There is a small admission charge to the reserve itself, which is open daily from dawn to dusk. Near by is the restored Fen Cottage, and a lovely thatched boathouse where the reserve's traditional working fen boat is kept. To return to the car park and village, simply walk back up the lane past the houses.

# A Pilgrim's Progress Through Ampthill

*Step out in John Bunyan's Bedfordshire around the elegant Georgian town of Ampthill.*

---

**DISTANCE** *7 miles (11.3km)*   **MINIMUM TIME** *3hrs 30min*

**ASCENT/GRADIENT** *607ft (185m)* ▲▲▲   **LEVEL OF DIFFICULTY** +++

**PATHS** *Variety of field paths, farm tracks and lanes, 3 stiles*

**LANDSCAPE** *Low greensand ridges, gentle, rolling farmland and woods*

**SUGGESTED MAP** *OS Explorer 193 Luton & Stevenage*

**START/FINISH** *Grid reference: TL 034381*

**DOG FRIENDLINESS** *On lead near livestock, good on enclosed tracks*

**PARKING** *Free car park off Church Street, Ampthill*

**PUBLIC TOILETS** *At car park*

---

Ampthill gained its charter for a weekly market as far back as 1219, and its park was used by Henry VIII for hunting (Catherine of Aragon lived in a castle here during their divorce). However, most of the fine period buildings that surround the Market Place and line Church Street, in particular, date from the late 18th and early 19th centuries. Ampthill's location on a prominent greensand ridge made it a popular stop-off for travellers on coaching routes, while today it's more notable for an inordinate number of antique shops.

To the north, and just off the walk, is Houghton House, built in 1615 for the Countess of Pembroke and systematically dismantled and emptied 179 years later by the Duke of Bedford. The shell of what must have been a fine building is still worth inspecting, especially as the views across the county from its open hilltop location are first rate.

## Bunyan's Spiritual Purpose

Houghton House was supposedly the inspiration for 'House Beautiful', and a nearby stretch of Bedford Road the 'Hill Difficulty', in John Bunyan's *Pilgrim's Progress*. This famous work of spiritual allegory, an ostensibly simple tale of a pilgrim's daily encounters as he wanders through the local countryside, was first published in 1678, since when it has been translated into more languages than any other book except the Bible (the John Bunyan Museum at Bedford has more than 170 translations).

John Bunyan was born in 1628 at Elstow, near Bedford, the son of a tinker, and initially followed in his father's footsteps. But seeking deeper, more spiritual explanations about heaven and earth he turned to the newly formed independent religious congregations that were springing up around Bedford. When laws were passed in an attempt to thwart the dissenting congregations, Bunyan refused to comply and was jailed for continuing to deliver public sermons.

He spent the next 12 years in prison, during which time he wrote a prolific amount of papers and books, including the *Pilgrim's Progress*, and on release spent the rest of his days preaching and public speaking.

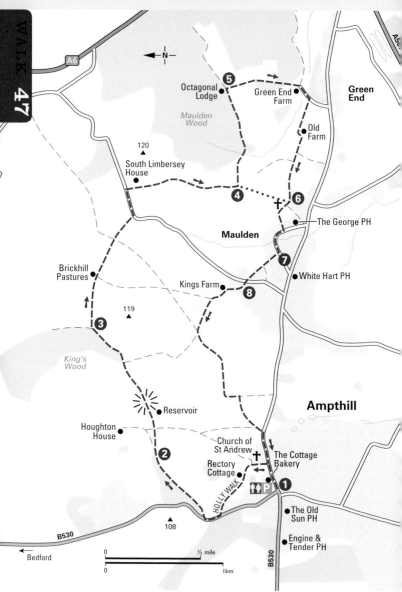

## WALK 47 DIRECTIONS

**1** From the Market Square in the centre of Ampthill walk east along Church Street and left to reach the handsome Church of St Andrew. Go along Rectory Lane, to its left and, at the end, go left through a gap by Rectory Cottage for the lovely Holly Walk. At the far end

cross the road and turn right. Walk up the pavement and, at the top of the bend, cross back over to join a concrete lane opposite.

**2** To visit the remains of Houghton House fork left by some houses, otherwise fork right to the reservoir gates where you switch to the farm track the other side of the hedge. Walk along this panoramic hilltop track to King's Wood, a locally run nature reserve. Go through the gate to the right and follow the path around the edge of the wood (or there is a parallel path through the trees if you prefer).

**3** After 0.25 mile (400m) turn right for a wide track that crosses first open fields, then Brickhill Pastures farmyard, then follows its drive to the lane at the end. Go left and, just before the turning for South Limbersey House, turn right on a public footpath across the field just to the right of the buildings. Follow this across and down to a kissing gate, then along a field-edge path to go through another gate.

**4** If you want to shorten the route by 1.5 miles (2.4km) go straight on to reach Maulden church, otherwise turn left through a further gate for a shady path to Maulden Wood. At the junction of tracks by its entrance turn first right for a clear bridleway that ends up skirting the southern edge of the woodland on an undulating fenced route.

**5** At the eye-catching octagonal lodge (private) turn right and walk along the track via a picnic area with wooden sculptures, and all the way down to join the surfaced lane at the bottom by Green End Farm. After 220yds (201m) go up the steps in the grassy embankment on the right for a waymarked route around the right-hand side of Old Farm. Bear left beyond the farmhouse to continue through fields, cross the end of a drive and another short field to reach St Mary's Church at Maulden.

**6** Follow the surfaced path out of the far side of the churchyard (the wide black gate beyond the mausoleum) and down to the road. Turn right to walk along George Street through Maulden.

**7** After 300yds (274m), just before Cobbitts Road, turn right along a narrow walkway between houses. Where it veers left, go straight on past the end of a house to reach the road, and cross over.

**8** Continue through fields, to the left of Kings Farm and, at the end of a narrow fenced enclosure, go along a short green lane. Turn left at the junction of routes at the end, and after following successive field-edges bend left on a track and, just before a ruined barn, turn right for a path that eventually drops down to Gas House Lane. Go left, then right to follow the main road back into Ampthill.

# Work Up an Appetite at Harrold-Odell

*Enjoy a day out at a country park north of Bedford, with a tasty reward.*

DISTANCE 4 miles (6.4km)  MINIMUM TIME 2hrs

ASCENT/GRADIENT 197ft (60m) ▲▲▲  LEVEL OF DIFFICULTY ✦✦✦

PATHS Park tracks, field-edges and woodland paths, 3 stiles

LANDSCAPE Open park with lakes by River Great Ouse, hilly woodland

SUGGESTED MAP OS Explorer 208 Bedford & St Neots

START/FINISH Grid reference: SP 956566

DOG FRIENDLINESS On lead in country park (not allowed in nature sanctuary)

PARKING Country park car park, near Harrold

PUBLIC TOILETS Visitor centre by car park

Harrold-Odell Country Park is located about 10 miles (16.1km) north-west of Bedford, between the attractive villages of Harrold and Odell. At the heart of the park are two shallow lakes, close to the banks of the River Great Ouse, which Bedfordshire County Council purchased around 20 years ago, and now the 144 acres (58ha) are a magnet for wildlife with as many as 160 species of birds recorded.

The visitor centre (open daily) by the main car park sports a well-stocked café and a small room full of information and exhibits concerning the park – from feathers and fossils through to ancient pottery and owl pellets – with a strong emphasis on resources to educate and entertain children.

## Of Lakes and Lagoons

The larger of the two lakes is known as Grebe Lake and not surprisingly is popular with wildfowl. Sometimes there can be literally hundreds of Canada and greylag geese honking fit to burst. Off the lakeside track on the southern shore you can visit a birdwatching hide, which tends to make ornithology a much more comfortable affair. The nature sanctuary, towards the north eastern corner of the park, is a pleasant area of reed-filled lagoons surrounded by willow and alder and offers a more secluded habitat favoured by the likes of newts and water voles.

Between the sanctuary and the River Great Ouse is a long strip of water-meadows which regularly flood in winter and early spring, and can be very heavy going after persistent rain. When this is the case stick to the firm gravel track around the main lake.

## The Bedfordshire Clanger

No, this is not one of those curious little pink space creatures from children's TV, but in fact a local delicacy once prepared by Bedfordshire women for their menfolk, who worked all day in the fields – and not dissimilar in that respect to the Cornish pasties originally made for Cornish tin miners. The Bedfordshire Clanger was formerly a boiled suet roll, but has now evolved into a baked suet crust and resembles a traditional pasty. It was designed

WALK 48

# HARROLD-ODELL COUNTRY PARK

to be a complete meal, with approximately two thirds containing savoury meat (usually stewing beef or bacon) with diced potato and chopped onion, while the other third was filled with a sweet ingredient like jam.

Sadly there are few places left that still make Clangers, but if you're exploring the county visit Sandy, east of Bedford, where Gunns Bakery still produce this unique all-in-one meal.

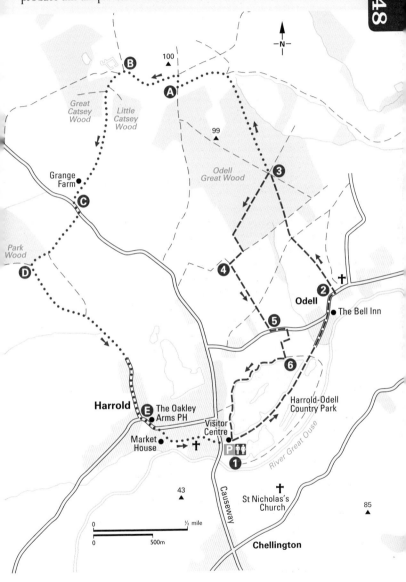

## WALK 48 DIRECTIONS

❶ Leave the car park by the visitor centre and walk to the far end of the park beyond the main

lake – either along the semi-surfaced path between the two lakes or across the long meadow by the side of the River Great Ouse (which may be difficult after heavy rain). Go through the gate at the far end of the main track and along the lane to the pub at Odell, with its riverside garden. Beyond this join the pavement of the High Street on a rising bend and cross over at the top, before you reach the church.

**2** Go through the double gate on the left for the public bridleway – not the footpath further on beside the church. Follow the wide grassy track uphill between the fields, ignoring all paths and tracks off left and right, and follow this broad and direct route into Odell Great Wood. After 0.25 mile (400m) of woodland walking you reach a major junction of routes.

> ### WHERE TO EAT AND DRINK
> Tea-Zels café at the visitor centre serves all-day breakfasts, sandwiches, panini, soup, jacket potatoes and delicious home-made cakes. The produce is always fresh and appetising, with meals cooked to order and good-value daily specials. For food-serving pubs, The Bell at Odell is a highly rated thatched pub with a pleasant riverside garden, and in Harrold visit The Oakley Arms (closed Monday).

**3** Turn first left, almost back on yourself, for a public footpath (indicated on a nearby waymarked post) through the trees to the south-western edge of the wood. Turn left and walk along the perimeter to the end, then don't go through the inviting gap in the hedge, but turn right through a metal gate to follow the field-edge to the far corner.

**4** Turn left and go over a high stile to follow a series of field-edges gradually downhill to the road at the bottom – and admire the pleasant views over the country park and river valley as

> ### WHILE YOU'RE THERE
> A wander into nearby Harrold is highly recommended – there's a path through the churchyard opposite the main entrance of the park. On the green is a small circular stone lock-up, where local miscreants would be held. Also take a look at the 11-arched medieval bridge and causeway that links Harrold to Chellington and Carlton.

you do so. St Nicholas's Church, isolated on a hilltop on the far side of the river, is particularly prominent, and a little to the west is the 14th-century tower of St Peter's Church at Harrold. The final field is a narrow, enclosed grassy strip used by local stables.

**5** Cross over the road and turn left to walk along the pavement. In 150yds (137m) go right, down through a wide field opening, and follow the right-hand side of the field as it zig-zags around to the far corner.

**6** Re-enter the country park and turn right on to the semi-surfaced path that skirts the northern side of the main lake. At the far end either walk along the grassy strip back to the visitor centre or follow the path into woodland by the road, and turn left for a short and shady track back to the start.

> ### WHAT TO LOOK FOR
> Odell Great Wood and Park Wood are both attractive mixed woods that support a range of wildlife, and in particular muntjac deer. These shy, tiny creatures (with a shoulder height of only 16in/40cm) have a dark red coat with white markings on the throat, chin and rump. They are not native to Britain, having escaped from parks and estates, but have now established themselves in wooded areas across the country.

# A Hike to Harrold

*Create a more demanding walk via*
*the fascinating village of Harrold.*
**See map and information panel for Walk 48**

---

**DISTANCE** *6 miles (9.7km)*  **MINIMUM TIME** *3hrs*
**ASCENT/GRADIENT** *311ft (95m)* ▲▲▲  **LEVEL OF DIFFICULTY** +++

---

## WALK 49 DIRECTIONS (Walk 48 option)

This extension incorporates part of a route devised by Bedfordshire County Council's Countryside Team, who produce an attractive series of walking trails.

A word of warning, however, the disued airfield north of Odell Great Wood now houses the Santa Pod Raceway, and at certain weekends in the year the incredibly loud vehicles roar up and down the main strip. They tend to practise on Saturday and race on Sunday, and if you're after a peaceful day out this is not the place to be.

At Point ❸ go straight over the junction of routes and follow the wide, straight forest ride to reach the wood's northern edge and out across a field. Turn left along the unsurfaced Yelnow Lane, which becomes a rough concrete track, then go across an open scrapyard to reach a junction (Point ❹). Turn right, signposted 'Podington' and, in a few paces, go left on to a wide concrete drive. This curves around the edge of the former Second-World-War airfield, from where American Flying Fortresses took off on daylight bombing raids.

Turn first left (Point ❺) across a wooden barrier, and keep left to follow an overgrown concrete track to the left-hand side of a fence. This becomes a fenced track that heads down between Great and Little Catsey Woods. Follow the waymarks across a field and around the left-hand side of Grange Farm's boundary fence to reach the road (Point ❻).

Turn left and in 175yds (160m) go right to reach a footpath up successive field-edges and alongside Park Wood as far as a dense hedge (Point ❼).

Turn left, and walk the broad track along the right-hand field-edge all the way down to the houses of Harrold, eventually joining a lane beyond the allotments. At the main road in the village centre turn left (Point ❽), passing The Oakley Arms and staying on the main road as it bends right, then left.

Go half right across the green, past the tiny circular lock-up and row of thatched cottages to reach a walkway that soon bears left to join a pavement, that crosses the approach to the church, and finally returns to the country park visitor centre via the churchyard.

# The Splendour of Wimpole

*An enjoyable ramble around the landscaped
grounds of a country mansion.*

**WALK 50**

---

**DISTANCE** *3 miles (4.8km)*    **MINIMUM TIME** *1hr 30min*

**ASCENT/GRADIENT** *213ft (65m)* ▲▲▲    **LEVEL OF DIFFICULTY** ✦✦✦

**PATHS** *Easy tracks and open park*

**LANDSCAPE** *Elegant landscaped parkland*

**SUGGESTED MAP** *OS Explorer 209 Cambridge*

**START/FINISH** *Grid reference: TL 338509*

**DOG FRIENDLINESS** *Keep on close lead around grazing sheep and cows*

**PARKING** *Wimpole Hall car park (pay-and-display)*

**PUBLIC TOILETS** *Wimpole Hall (converted stable block)*

---

## WALK 50 DIRECTIONS

Wimpole Hall is among the National Trust's most impressive properties, an 18th-century mansion surrounded by 350 acres (142ha) of landscaped lakes, follies and woodland. Despite its original splendour, the house passed through several different owners and by the early 20th century was in a poor condition. In 1938 it was bought by Captain George Bambridge whose wife, Elsie, was the daughter of Rudyard Kipling. After her husband's death she continued its gradual restoration, and when she died in 1976 the house and entire estate were left to the National Trust.

On the corner where the public driveway reaches the main car park, take the gate in the black railings for a path that runs diagonally across two open fields towards Home Farm. Aim just to the left of the red telephone box on the lane on the far side.

Turn left into the lane and walk past the farm and on past Thornberry Hill Cottages at Brick End. About 350yds (320m) beyond a small humpback bridge, at the far side of Nursery Plantation, turn left through a double-gated track. Carry on through another gate and out into open fields, and follow the fence around the top of the slope.

On your right, but out of bounds, is a curious hilltop folly resembling the ruins of a small castle. It was built in the late 1760s – deliberately as a ruin. Commissioned by the 1st Earl of Hardwicke, Lord Chancellor at the time, the sham castle was purely an aesthetic feature, designed to be viewed from the front and right (in other words from Wimpole Hall itself). It was designed by Sanderson Miller, who spent a lifetime designing Gothic castles, prospect towers and castellated ruins, and perhaps not surprisingly suffered from periodic bouts of madness. Its building was overseen by the ubiquitous Lancelot Brown, a leading exponent of what was referred to as the 'Natural Landscape', and who acquired his nickname 'Capability' because of his assertion that every park was 'capable of improvement'.

---

**WHAT TO LOOK FOR**

Wimpole Hall stands in a classically landscaped English park, with grand tree-lined avenues, serpentine lakes and bizarre follies, as well as a ha-ha (a trench that separates the garden from the parkland without impeding the view).

---

Just beyond the folly, turn left and, enjoying the fine views across to the hall, walk down across the open hillside to the lakes at the bottom of the slope.

Go over the Chinese bridge, built in 1767 and restored in 1986, and on towards the back of the hall that is just visible above the brow of the hill. Cross the iron bridge and, approaching the gardens by the hall, swing right to reach the gate beyond the curving railings. Go through the gate and turn right to walk sharply uphill along the grassy, tree-lined avenue. It originally comprised elm, but following the ravages of Dutch elm disease it was replanted with lime.

At the very top turn left and, with the hall away to your left, walk downhill on a clear path through the rough grassland alongside a fence (which is on your right). Ahead are expansive views over Hertfordshire towards the distant Chilterns. At the bottom of the slope turn left on to the surfaced drive and follow this back to the turning for the main

approach to the hall. The former stable block, which now houses the information point, as well as refreshments and toilets, is a little further along the driveway.

Wimpole Hall was designed by James Gibbs, Henry Flitcroft and Sir John Soane, and contains some notable features, not least the stunning Yellow Drawing Room and the Bath House with its 2,000-gallon (9,092-litre) plunge bath. The library was built in 1730 to hold part of the former owner's, Lord Harley, massive collection of books, and such was his literary and artistic standing that visitors to Wimpole included Alexander Pope and Jonathan Swift. More recent rooms include Mrs Bambridge's study, dressing room and bedroom, all on show with period items and original furnishings.

Adjoining the hall is Wimpole Home Farm, open daily (except Thursday and Friday) from March to October, weekends at other times. Built in 1794 and carefully restored by the National Trust, it's now home to a diverse range of rare breeds that were common in previous centuries, including Longhorn cattle, Soay sheep and Tamworth pigs. Not surprisingly, it's immensely popular with children. The enormous Great Barn houses a fascinating display of farm machinery and implements dating back over 200 years.

Wimpole Hall is usually open from the beginning of March until the end of October (closed Thursday and Friday, except Thursdays during school holidays), while the park is open daily from sunrise to sunset all year round.

WALK 50

# Walking in Safety

All these walks are suitable for any reasonably fit person, but less experienced walkers should try the easier walks first. Route finding is usually straightforward, but you will find that an Ordnance Survey map is a useful addition to the route maps and descriptions.

## RISKS

Although each walk here has been researched with a view to minimising the risks to the walkers who follow its route, no walk in the countryside can be considered to be completely free from risk. Walking in the outdoors will always require a degree of common sense and judgement to ensure that it is as safe as possible.

- Be particularly careful on cliff paths and in upland terrain, where the consequences of a slip can be very serious.

- Remember to check tidal conditions before walking on the seashore.

- Some sections of route are by, or cross, busy roads. Take care and remember traffic is a danger even on minor country lanes.

- Be careful around farmyard machinery and livestock, especially if you have children with you.

- Be aware of the consequences of changes in the weather and check the forecast before you set out. Carry spare clothing and a torch if you are walking in the winter months. Remember the weather can change very quickly at any time of the year, and in moorland and heathland areas, mist and fog can make route finding much harder. Don't set out in these conditions unless you are confident of your navigation skills in poor visibility. In summer remember to take account of the heat and sun; wear a hat and carry spare water.

- On walks away from centres of population you should carry a whistle and survival bag. If you do have an accident requiring the emergency services, make a note of your position as accurately as possible and dial 999.

## COUNTRYSIDE CODE

- Be safe, plan ahead and follow any signs.

- Leave gates and property as you find them.

- Protect plants and animals and take your litter home.

- Keep dogs under close control.

- Consider other people.

For more information visit www.countrysideaccess.gov.uk/things_to_know/countryside_code